TIMBER,

TALUS &

TUNDRA

By Mary Anne Tarr
with
Illustrations by Abigail Tarr

Hiking Trails & Mountain Peaks
of the
Gunnison Basin

UNCOMPAHGRE BOOKS

Happy Hiking
Mary Anne Tarr

All photos taken by author unless otherwise noted.
All maps made by author from USGS Maps in Public Domain

Front Cover: This is the beautiful campsite up Matterhorn Creek at the entrance to the basin below Matterhorn Peak.

Back Cover: Large photo was taken by Sean McCormick on the 20 mile hike with BSA Troop #476. The hikers are above Conundrum Hot Springs in the Conundrum Creek drainage. Top inset is Amanda Tarr at Lost Lake. Bottom photo is Carolyn Thompson approaching the summit of Avery Peak.

Dedication Page: Old Man of the Mountains Sunflowers nestled amongst Alpine Forget-Me-Nots on Middle Baldy Mountain.

ATTENTION HIKERS

The information in this book is based on the author's experiences in the backcountry of the Gunnison Basin. Trails can be significantly altered through the power of wind, rain or avalanches. Do not rely solely on the information in this book; always carry a map and compass. The purpose of this book is to suggest hiking trails or routes, not to provide instruction for the user. There is no substitute for knowledge and experience to help ensure safety in the backcountry.

UNCOMPAHGRE BOOKS
1084 Seneca Drive
Gunnison, CO 81230

Library of Congress Catalog Card Number: 96-90018
ISBN 0-9650842-0-5

Printed in the United States of America
Wendell's Print Shop

ACKNOWLEDGMENTS

Hiking: My thanks go to all the folks who have accompanied me on these hikes over the years, and especially during the summer of 1995. I am especially grateful to my husband, John, who went on numerous hikes with me this past summer. I have enjoyed hiking and climbing with my husband and three children for over twenty years. Thanks also go to my friend, Anne Ash, for going with me on numerous explorations. Special thanks go to my friend and parish priest, Fr. Jim Koenigsfeld, with whom I have climbed almost all of the peaks in this book on our Tuesday parish outings. Cyr Pelletier, who passed away in August of 1995, was a climbing friend from these outings and his presence is sadly missed by all. Nancy Ruehle and Donna Rozman have also been on so many of these hikes with me. Thanks go to many friends who went with me this past summer: Ruth Bains, Eric & Pat Fullmer, Sarah Garcia, Diane & Tim Kruse, Kevin Irwin, Laura McClow, Becca & Diane McCormick, Sean McCormick and Boy Scout Troop #476, Thea Nordling, Amy Pabst, Mary Pavillard, Debbie Sporcich, Carolyn, Cole, Josh, Risto & Skye Thompson, Nancy Vogel, and Steven Wells.

History: I am very grateful to Dr. Duane Vandenbusche, WSC Professor of History, author and local historian, for reviewing the historical accuracy of my book. His expertise in local history is invaluable.

Geology: Many thanks go to Dr. Thomas Prather, WSC Professor of Geology and author, who helped me considerably with understanding the geology of the area.

Fishing: Information about fishing was provided to me by Jerry Piquette, a longtime Gunnison resident who spends as much time as possible hiking and fishing in our beautiful outdoors. Philip Mason of the Lake City Division of Wildlife assisted with fishing information for the Lake City area. My thanks go to both Jerry and Phil for their help.

Editing: This book contains far fewer errors thanks to three people who were kind enough to spend their time reading, editing and proofing: Fr. Jim Koenigsfeld, Susan Lebow, and Diane McCormick. Also my thanks go to Marva Craig for allowing me the use of her laser printer.

This book is dedicated to the memory of
Two Old Men of the Mountains:

Eli H. Worden
My father and friend

Cyr Pelletier
My mountain climbing friend

You are remembered,
On high mountain peaks,
In the timber and the tundra.
Power and fragile beauty joined
In engulfing vastness.
God embraces.
Nature reassures;
We will meet again.

TABLE OF CONTENTS

Ohio Creek Valley

Curecanti and the West Elks

Lake City Area

ILLUSTRATIONS

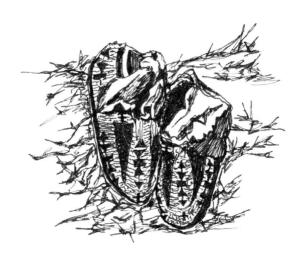

Empty Moccasins

INTRODUCTION

Go placidly amid the noise and haste, and remember what peace there may be in silence....You are a child of the universe, no less than the trees and the stars; you have a right to be here. And whether or not it is clear to you, no doubt the universe is unfolding as it should. Therefore, be at peace with God, whatever you conceive Him to be, and whatever your labors and aspirations, in the noisy confusion of life keep peace with your soul. With all its sham, drudgery and broken dreams, it is still a beautiful world. Be careful. Strive to be happy.

--Desiderata

...remember what peace there may be in silence. Remember the walk in the wilderness, filled with quiet beauty and solitude. Remember the gentle sound of the wind rustling in the trees. Remember the joyful song of a forest bird, the high squeak of a pika or the whistle of a marmot resonating across the talus. Remember the fragile beauty of even the smallest wildflower. Remember the privilege of being a guest in the high alpine environment. Remember the summits. Remember and be at peace.

In setting parameters for the hikes in this book, I remembered my walks in the high, wild places. These thoughts led me, with only a few exceptions, to hikes in designated wilderness areas, free from motorized and mechanized vehicles. For convenience of the traveler, all hikes and/or backpack trips start and end at the same place and require only one vehicle. In addition, the hikes begin from a location accessible to most passenger cars. All hikes in this book are non-technical.

Although I recommend the USGS Maps (7.5 minute series) for topographical detail when hiking, there have been many changes in the wilderness designations in the Gunnison Country which are not reflected on these maps. Anyone going into the backcounrty should know where these wilderness areas are located and what rules govern them. The local Forest Service Office can provide information about these areas.

INTRODUCTION

The Gunnison Basin contains many fascinating remnants of Colorado's historical inhabitants. There is even some evidence of ancient peoples which has been found near Gunnison. In more recent history, this territory was first home to the Ute Indians, who wandered freely and made their camps, although they left the least evidence of their presence. Next came explorers, trappers, miners and railroad builders, with the greatest influx of people occurring in the 1880's when the mining boom brought thousands who sought their fortunes in gold and silver. It is awesome to think about the lives and the hardships of all these earlier inhabitants. They went places most of us would never think of going in the winter, much less living. Many did not survive. They constructed amazing things, all by hand, using picks, shovels, dynamite, mules and wagons. It is unfortunate that many of our mountains have been left forever scarred, but with this lies our history and the shattered dreams of many who lived here before us.

Climbing Colorado's 14,000' peaks has become a very popular endeavor for many people. During the summer of 1994, while working on Uncompahgre Peak, I counted 1007 names on the summit register in a 6 week period. Even though the Gunnison country has several of these popular peaks, I have chosen not to give their route descriptions as there are already three excellent guides available. And, more importantly, there are so many other magnificent mountains in this area which can be climbed and which do not have such intensive impact on their delicate tundra. As more and more people choose to spend their free time hiking, camping and mountain climbing in the Colorado backcountry, it is essential to treasure our resources. This book encompasses the beautiful and diverse country of the Gunnison Basin, bounded with high mountain peaks, several towering to above 14,000', and nourished by the many lakes and streams draining into the Gunnison River. Our Gunnison country is a fragile environment and it is my hope that users of this guide will be gentle with the land and help to protect and nurture this environment so it will last for generations to come.

We have not inherited the earth from our fathers,
We are borrowing it from our children.
                                          --Native American Saying

HIKING HINTS

CLOTHING

Even though it seems very warm or even hot in the towns and valleys, when in the mountains, a clear morning can turn into a cloudy, rainy afternoon, with snow possible in the higher elevations. Before entering the high country, hikers and climbers should be prepared for these weather changes. Hypothermia can happen at any time of the year at high elevations. I would recommend always taking a jacket, some means of rain protection, a pair of gloves and a hat. If you are going above treeline and plan to wear shorts, carry a pair of long underwear or windpants as a backup for unexpected cold. Dressing in layers makes it easier to stay comfortable by shedding or adding one layer of clothing at a time. I definitely recommend investing in a pair of hiking boots. The tread on hiking boots provides much better traction than on other types of shoes, especially on descents. It's no fun to slip and fall, and your chances can be lessened with appropriate footwear.

As a special note, during the Big Game Rifle Season which occurs in October and November, hordes of hunters flock to the Gunnison backcountry. If you care to risk hiking during this time, wear lots of blaze orange and make plenty of people noise to lessen your chance of being mistaken for a deer or elk. And remember it is possible for a bullet which misses its mark to zing through the air for up to one half mile!

EQUIPMENT

I always carry a backpack, but some of the fanny packs available today can carry sufficient amounts for day hikes. I recommend carrying a map of the area and a compass, especially when off-trail hiking. Sunburn occurs more easily at high elevations, and it is important to protect your skin with sunscreen and your eyes with sunglasses. A flashlight or headlamp are good to have in an emergency. Minimal first aid items like bandaids and moleskin (for blisters) should be included in your supplies.

FOOD/WATER

It is very important to carry liquids with you. In many places there is no water available. Water from the streams or lakes should not be consumed without first using some means of purification. In order to be prepared for the unexpected, always take some food along, even on a short hike.

WEATHER

Thunderstorms can occur anytime during the summer, and are most likely to occur in the afternoons during July and August. During a thunderstorm, it is important to stay off ridges and away from open areas in order to protect from lightning strikes. Hikes or climbs which go above treeline should be started early in the day to allow time to return to the timber before the afternoon storms. Try to be down by noon.

Avalanches can be a danger where there is snow, especially in early spring. If you plan to travel on snow, learn about the characteristics of snow and avalanches before going.

CHILDREN

Over the years of hiking with my own children, as well as many other young people through the Boy Scouts and family friends, I know how important it is to make hiking fun. Take time to experience nature and to play. Be flexible in reaching a specific destination. It is better to leave wanting more, rather than having had too much.

Safety Note: If you plan to glissade or hike on snowfields, carry an ice axe and learn about travel on snow. *Mountaineering, The Freedom of the Hills* by The Mountaineers, provides excellent information on snow and the use of an ice axe. Practice self-arrests with the ice axe in a controlled setting before trusting your life to it. Several people have died in the Colorado mountains when their glissading went out of control and sent them crashing into rocks.

Safety Note: Due to the presence of toxic gases in old mines, do not go in. **NEVER GO IN AN OLD MINE!!!**

USE OF THIS BOOK

The hikes in this book are grouped geographically by direction from Gunnison. The various roads used to reach trailheads are listed in outline form after the introduction to each section. When it is necessary to turn onto a new road, the subsequent directions are indented. Each hike is preceded by a template which includes the name of the hike, USGS maps, trailhead, starting elevation, total elevation gain, round trip distance, and a rating.

A formula was developed to provide an objective rating for each hike according to difficulty. In Appendix B is an explanation of this formula and a chart comparing all the hikes. The subjective factor which cannot be figured into the formula is each individual hiker. Physical fitness, age, acclimatization and experience all play a major role in a hiker's ability to successfully complete a hike.

Abbreviations found in this book are as follows:

CR County Road

FR Forest Service Road

USGS United States Geological Survey

TH Trailhead

SE Starting elevation

TVG Total vertical gain

RT Round trip

In Appendix A is an alphabetical listing, by common name, of all wildflowers and trees mentioned in this book. The common names, which vary, are followed by the Latin name.

There is no substitute for knowledge and experience in the backcountry. If you are new to the backcountry, consider taking someone who has knowledge and experience with you. The purpose of this book is not to teach, but rather to suggest available trails and routes in the Gunnison Basin. Even if you are experienced, do not hike alone. Always tell someone where you are hiking and when you expect to return.

This book is written for use in early summer through late fall. When the leaves fall off the aspens, the streams are covered with ice, and there is snow on the peaks, it is time to put this book away and get out your skis!

THE GUNNISON BASIN

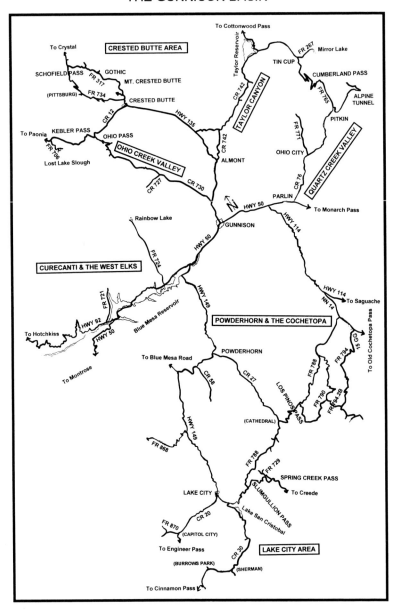

GUNNISON BASIN

So, what is the Gunnison Basin? Generally speaking, the Gunnison Basin refers to the lands with waters which drain into the Gunnison River. The hikes in this book lie within the Gunnison River drainage with just a couple of exceptions. The high mountain peaks of the San Juans around Lake City, Powderhorn and the Cochetopa feed into the Lake Fork of the Gunnison River. The far west portion of the Gunnison Basin is bounded by the mountains of the Continental Divide and the Sawatch Range. Closer to Gunnison, but still to the west, are the mountains of the Fossil Ridge Wilderness Area. These areas to the west ultimately drain into the Taylor River or Quartz Creek and Tomichi Creek and finally into the Gunnison River. To the north, drainage of the Elk and Ruby Ranges above Crested Butte is into the Slate and East Rivers, and the Anthracites and portions of the West Elks drain into Ohio Creek. The East River and the Taylor River join at Almont to form the Gunnison River. Finally to the west, the creeks of the West Elk Range flow into the reservoirs of the Gunnison River. The landscape changes west of town, going from high mountain peaks and mesas to a deep canyon carved by the Gunnison River--the Black Canyon of the Gunnison.

TOWN OF GUNNISON

Gunnison was named for Captain John W. Gunnison of the Army Topographical Engineers. Gunnison explored much of the Gunnison Basin looking for a transcontinental railroad route in 1853. He was killed by Indians in Utah on October 26 of the same year.

The community of Gunnison has been a major hub in the Gunnison Basin since the 1880's. It was the major supply town for the surrounding mining camps. In 1882, the first train rolled into Gunnison and spur tracks were soon laid out of Gunnison to the other communities. Western State College began as the Colorado State Normal School in 1911. Today, jets fly in and out of the Gunnison Airport, carrying skiers bound for Crested Butte. Tourists congregate at Blue Mesa Reservoir and radiate out to surrounding areas for additional recreation.

Significant numbers of hunters use Gunnison as a base of operations during the fall hunting season.

Since all of the major areas covered in this book surround the city of Gunnison and comprise the Gunnison Basin, Gunnison will serve as the hub for this hiking guide. All of the hikes can be easily reached from Gunnison.

NORTH

28 miles north of Gunnison via Highway 135 is the Crested Butte region which encompasses portions of the Elk Mountains in the Maroon Bells-Snowmass Wilderness. Most of the rocks in the Elk Mountains are sedimentary from the Paleozoic and Mesozoic ages. However, there are some very interesting igneous intrusions of white granite which were pushed up during the Cenozoic age. Of particular notice in the Crested Butte area are four laccoliths, igneous intrusions of magma which push up the sedimentary strata, and which have a flat base and a dome shaped top. These laccoliths are Round Mountain, Crested Butte Mountain, Snodgrass and Gothic Mountain.

Ohio Creek Valley begins just 3 miles northwest of Gunnison at the intersection of Highway 135 and Ohio Creek Road (CR 730). This valley has access into the West Elk Wilderness and the Gunnison National Forest and also leads to the Ruby Range in the Raggeds Wilderness near Crested Butte. There are more laccoliths to be seen while driving up the Ohio Creek Valley -- Whetstone Mountain, Mt. Axtell, Carbon Peak and the Anthracites. The Ruby Range is noted for its igneous intrusions of magma known as dikes and sills.

WEST

Lying 9 miles west of Gunnison on Highway 50 is the Curecanti National Recreation Area comprised of Blue Mesa, Morrow Point and Crystal Reservoirs. Also west of Gunnison are many access roads to the West Elk Wilderness, with Rainbow Lake Road (FR 724) and Soap Creek Road (FR 721) being the ones in this book.

The area west of Gunnison has some fascinating geological history. About 30 million years ago, there was a large volcano in the area of what is today, West Elk Peak. Much of the volcanic debris, known as West Elk Breccia, was transported by huge mudflows which then, through erosion, left the breccia standing in spires like the Dillon Pinnacles. A bit closer to this old volcano site in the Ohio Creek area, are the pinnacles of Mill Creek and the Castles.

The spectacular Black Canyon of the Gunnison also has interesting geological history in that the Gunnison River chose its course through some hard and very resistant Precambrian rocks because they were covered by softer volcanic rocks. If the harder rocks had not been covered by these softer rocks, most likely the Gunnison River would have chosen its path a bit further south.

SOUTH

This book covers a large, interconnected area comprised of the Cochetopa, the Powderhorn Valley extending along Cebolla Creek, and the Lake City Area. The Cochetopa is reached via Highways 50 and 114 in approximately 28 miles. The Cochetopa is joined to the Powderhorn Valley by FR 790 which leads over Los Pinos Pass. Powderhorn is also reached in 26 miles from Gunnison via Highways 50 and 149. Lake City can be reached from Powderhorn via the Cebolla Creek Road which intersects the Slumgullion Pass Road. Highways 50 and 149 from Gunnison reach Lake City in 54 miles.

The Cochetopa is in Gunnison National Forest and the La Garita Wilderness. The public lands around Powderhorn are the Powderhorn Wilderness (formerly the Powderhorn Primitive Area) managed by the BLM, and the La Garita Wilderness and Gunnison National Forest managed by the U.S. Forest Service. North of Lake City is the Uncompahgre Wilderness (formerly the Big Blue Wilderness) and Uncompahgre National Forest. South of Lake City is a BLM Wilderness Study Area up the Lake Fork Valley. Finally, the area east of Lake City near Slumgullion Pass is La Garita Wilderness. The mountains in this area are part of the San Juan Mountains.

Somewhere between 10 and 30 million years ago, the Northern San Juans were also volcanic. This area was comprised of many volcanos, instead of just one as in the West Elks. The area has evidence of 15 calderas, large circular depressions formed by the collapse of a volcano following gigantic eruptions of volcanic ash. Quite frequently really unusual rocks can be found in the mountains of this area, providing evidence of the volcanic ash. The mesas around Blue Mesa Reservoir are also the result of eruptions in the San Juans, and their hard rocky tops are known as welded tuffs, formed from ash fragments which were welded together at very high temperatures during eruptions.

EAST

The areas east of Gunnison are the Quartz Creek Valley and Taylor Canyon. The Quartz Creek Valley is reached via Highway 50 and CR 76, 12 miles from Gunnison at Parlin. The intersection of Highway 135 and CR 742, 10 miles north of Gunnison at Almont is the start of Taylor Canyon. The Quartz Creek Valley and Taylor Canyon are also joined by Cumberland Pass above Taylor Reservoir.

The Quartz Creek Valley contains the Fossil Ridge Wilderness which lies east of Gunnison. Further to the east the Gunnison Basin is bounded by the Sawatch Range, which is an uplift of Precambrian rock. Coming west from the Sawatch Range, there are Lower Paleozoic formations over the Precambrian rocks. Fossil Ridge is an example of this and is composed of Lower Paleozoic carbonates which have many fossils.

CRESTED BUTTE AREA

The town of Crested Butte, with silver and gold mines to the north in the high mountains, rests on beds of coal. These coal beds were heavily mined and extended to Floresta near the top of Kebler Pass and out into the Slate River Valley. The "Big Mine", owned by Colorado Fuel and Iron, was located right in town, and now there are maintained nordic ski tracks and several private homes on the old mine property. Although the "Big Mine" closed in 1952, Crested Butte struggled along, to be revived when a ski area was started by Dick Eflin and Fred Rice during the winter of 1962-63. Today that ski area has grown to become Crested Butte Mountain Resort.

Trailheads and roads heading west from Crested Butte on the Kebler Pass Road are the following distances from the 4-way stop on Highway 135 in Crested Butte:

Ohio Pass Road is 9 miles
Lost Lake turnoff (FR 706) is 16.9 miles
Lost Lake Slough Campground is 18.9 miles

Trailheads and roads heading north from Crested Butte on the Gothic Road are the following distances from the 4-way stop on Highway 135 in Crested Butte:

Slate River Road is .8 mile
Crested Butte Mountain Resort is 2.6 miles
Gothic General Store is 7.9 miles

SLATE RIVER VALLEY

Slate River Road (FR 734) is .8 miles north of the 4-way stop in Crested Butte towards the ski area and turns off to the left. On the right side of the valley, located up on Smith Hill, was the second largest coal mine in the Crested Butte region. The left side of this valley had several silver mines up Oh-Be-Joyful Creek and Poverty Gulch. At the head of the valley, the road climbs to the top of Paradise Divide, overlooking Paradise Basin. Although many passenger cars are able to make the drive to the summit of Paradise Divide, be aware that this road is steep and narrow, and also rather exposed.

Trailheads and roads departing from the Slate River Road are the following distances from the intersection of the Slate River Road and the Gothic Road:

Gunsight Pass Road is 3.5 miles
Oh-Be-Joyful Road is 4.5 miles
Oh-Be-Joyful TH is 5 miles
Pittsburg sign is 6.5 miles
Poverty Gulch TH is 7.1 miles
Start of Paradise Divide Road is 8.9 miles
Top of Paradise Divide TH is 11.9 miles

Nellie, the Jeep, at the Oh-Be-Joyful turnoff on Slate River Road

GOTHIC VALLEY

The old mining town of Gothic had its boom in the early 1880's. Today it provides a campus for the Rocky Mountain Biological Laboratory (RMBL), established in 1928 by WSC professor, Dr. John C. Johnson. Many students and prominent professors come to the RMBL to do high altitude biological research in the summer. The road beyond Gothic was once the dangerous Schofield to Gothic Toll Road in the 1880's, and continuing from Schofield Pass over to Crystal is the road with a 27% grade down Crystal Canyon next to the famous Devil's Punchbowl.

CRESTED BUTTE AREA

Avery Peak and the Gothic Valley from Schofield Pass Road

Driving from Gothic to Emerald Lake, it is easy to see evidence of the huge avalanches in this valley. Many summers the road just before Emerald Lake remains blocked by an avalanche too large to clear. Some years, when the big avalanche runs off Gothic Mountain, the road is blocked immediately above Gothic until July. Imagine the danger and what it would have been like to travel this road in the winter! However, during the summer months, there are many great places to hike in the Gothic Valley.

The trailheads and roads are the following distances from the Gothic General Store:

Judd Falls Road is .6 miles
    Judd Falls TH is 1 mile
Avery Campground is 1.4 miles
Gothic Campground TH is 2.1 miles
Rustler's Gulch Road and TH is 2.6 miles
Emerald Lake is 5 miles
Schofield Pass is 5.5 miles
West Maroon TH is 6.3 miles

BECKWITH PASS 9900'
USGS Anthracite Range
TH Lost Lake Slough Campground
SE 9623'
TVG 300'
RT 5 miles
EASY TO MODERATE

Beckwith Pass is named for Lt. E. G. Beckwith, who was the assistant assigned to Capt. John W. Gunnison on his exploration of this area. Lt. Beckwith, left in charge of the main camp, did not accompany Capt. Gunnison on the fateful day of his death by hostile Indians in Utah.

The easiest walk (least elevation gain) to Beckwith Pass is from Lost Lake Slough Campground. Do not use the trailhead just before the campground as there is a better one ahead with a parking area nearby. Continue into the campground and turn left. The trailhead is at the end of the campground. It is approximately 2.6 miles to the summit of the pass through aspen, open meadows and a beautiful Blue Spruce and fir forest. This would be a beautiful fall hike as there are spacious views of the surrounding mountains, covered with aspen trees, on the return hike. At the summit of Beckwith Pass at 9920', walk about 100' east (left) for a beautiful view of the Castles. The trails are a bit confusing during the last .5 mile to the top of the pass. I would recommend the rightmost trail for the gentlest walk. The most predominant flower on this hike is the Lupine. This trail has heavy horse use. The lake at the campground supports Brook and Rainbow Trout.

LOST LAKE AND DOLLAR LAKE
USGS Anthracite Range
TH Lost Lake Slough Campground
SE 9623'
TVG 400'
RT 2.5 miles
EASY TO MODERATE

A very scenic circle hike can be taken from the Lost Lake Slough Campground to Lost Lake and Dollar Lake. The trailhead is near the entrance to the campground. Follow the trail for .6 mile up to pretty Lost Lake at 9870'. This lake has Brook and Rainbow Trout. After enjoying Lost Lake for awhile, hike up and around the base of East Beckwith Mountain to even smaller Dollar Lake at 10,020'. Dollar Lake has Emerald Lake Rainbow Trout for the fishing hikers. The trail continues beyond Dollar Lake for another mile down to join the Beckwith Pass Trail at its first stream crossing just above the campground. Try backpacking the short distance to Lost Lake with very young children. Our family did it, and it was wonderful.

Family backpacking trip to Lost Lake

LOST LAKE, DOLLAR LAKE & BECKWITH PASS

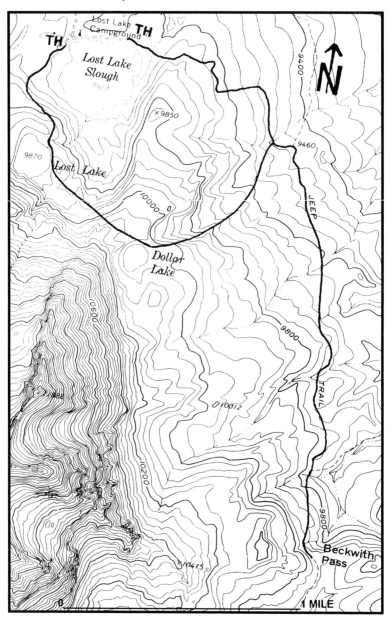

BLUE LAKE 11,055'
OH-BE-JOYFUL PASS 11,760'

USGS Oh-Be-Joyful

TH Oh-Be-Joyful camping area on Slate River Road

SE 9041'

TVG 2000' to Blue Lake

RT 11 miles

MODERATE TO STRENUOUS

TVG 2700' to Oh-Be-Joyful Pass

RT 13 miles

STRENUOUS

How could anything not be good? This is Oh-Be-Joyful. The trailhead for this hike is at the Slate River ford which is at the beginning of the Oh-Be-Joyful camping area up the Slate River Road. As with many streams and rivers of the Gunnison Basin, the Slate River can be very much a river during runoff and then dwindle to a gentle stream later in the season. After the ford, you will follow the old Oh-Be-Joyful Toll Road of the 1880's as it parallels the Gunsight Pass Road across the valley for the first mile and a half. After the first mile, you will come to the boundary of the Raggeds Wilderness Area, and all vehicles will be prohibited beyond. At this boundary, be sure to go to the right around the little fence section to remain on the main trail. The leading side of the first sharp peak you will probably notice is Peeler Peak, and you will pass it on your left while following Oh-Be-Joyful Creek up the valley. Peeler Peak is soon joined by Garfield Peak. There are several beautiful waterfalls cascading down from these peaks. Brook Trout swim in the water of Oh-Be-Joyful Creek. Evidence of the ravages of winter avalanches is also obvious throughout the valley. The trail passes through pine, spruce, fir and aspen, as well as open meadows filled with wildflowers. To the right of the trail, the high point on the long ridge is 12,146', Schuylkill Mountain.

At the head of the valley, the peaks coming into view are first, Hancock, then Oh-Be-Joyful, then Afley and finally,

Purple Peak. The trail is quite gentle and does not steepen until near the head of the valley, at which time it may seem like the trail is going to climb Oh-Be-Joyful Peak. However, right at the base of the peak, there is a trail junction, with the right fork leading into Democrat Basin and Oh-Be-Joyful Pass, and the left fork leading to Blue Lake, nestled below Purple Peak. Oh-Be-Joyful Pass can be seen from the main trail farther down the valley as the low spot between Hancock Peak and Richmond Peak, the peak which is a mile further on the ridge to the right of the pass. On the return down valley near Peeler Peak, there is a good view of the top of the Gunsight Pass Road.

To reach Blue Lake, continue on the left fork of the trail. At the top of the first rise, you can see the basin where the lake is located beneath Purple Peak, but will be unable to actually see the lake until you reach the basin. This lake is gorgeous, flanked by Purple and Afley Peaks on the one side and a meadow full of Colorado Columbine on the other. The meadow side of the lake is quite shallow, making it easy to see many fish, although the ones I saw were not very big. Blue Lake supports Snake River Cutthroat.

Across from Blue Lake, to the east, is a notch in the ridge just below Garfield Peak, which leads to Peeler Basin and Peeler Lakes. Many locals refer to this notch as Peeler Pass. It is but a short hike from the notch to the summit of Garfield Peak. From Blue Lake it is about 2.5 miles to Lower Peeler Lakes. It is possible also to reach Peeler Basin from the popular 4-wheel drive Gunsight Pass Road via Redwell Basin.

Blue Lake lies nestled in the basin below Purple Peak

DAISY PASS 11,600'
OH-BE-JOYFUL PASS 11,760'

USGS Oh-Be-Joyful

TH Poverty Gulch

SE 9200'

TVG 2400' to Daisy Pass

RT 6 miles

MODERATE TO STRENUOUS

TVG 3200' to Oh-Be-Joyful with 640' on return

RT 10 miles

VERY STRENUOUS

To hike to Daisy Pass, follow the directions for Augusta Mine as far as the intersection with the Daisy Pass Trail. Go left at the intersection as the road takes a switchback up the mountain side into Baxter Basin, which was named after 1880's miner, Yank Baxter. Baxter was the owner of the Excelsior Mine located at the head of Poverty Gulch, and was particularly well-known for his very loud voice. It is a steady climb up into the basin, after which the trail contours the basin for a bit until a steeper ascent up switchbacks to the summit of 11,600', Daisy Pass. Going to Daisy Pass provides a nice day hike.

The Daisy Pass hike can be lengthened by crossing Democrat Basin and hiking to the summit of Oh-Be-Joyful Pass at 11,760'. If this seems like too much for a day hike, consider dropping down to the trees in Democrat Basin and camping for a night.   From Oh-Be-Joyful Pass, 12,410', Hancock Peak, 12,400', Oh-Be-Joyful Peak, and 12,646', Afley Peak can be climbed to the south. The peaks in this area have a lot of rotten rock, and it would be wise to have some experience with this type of climbing before attempting these peaks.

BLUE LAKE & OH-BE-JOYFUL PASS

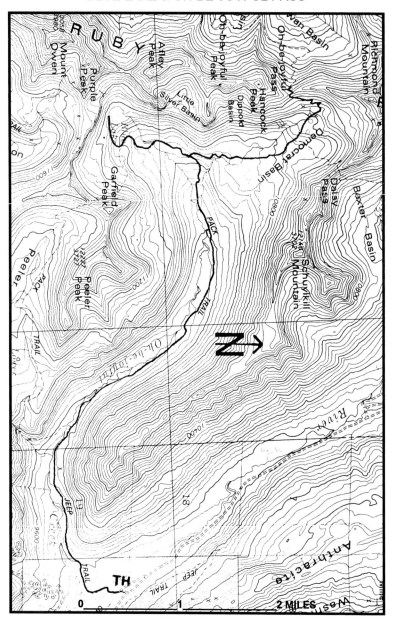

DAISY PASS & OH-BE-JOYFUL PASS

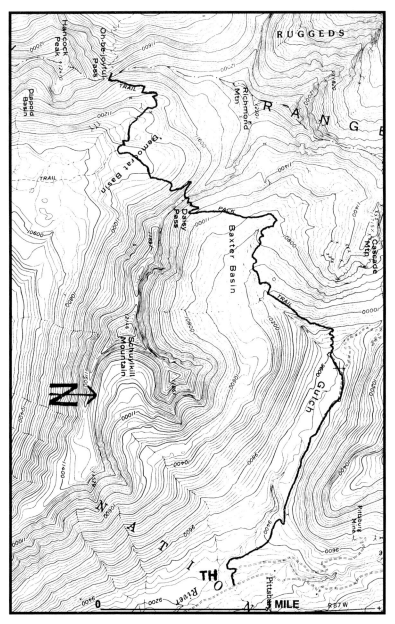

AUGUSTA MINE 11,000'
USGS Oh-Be-Joyful
TH Poverty Gulch
SE 9200'
TVG 1800'
RT 8 miles
MODERATE TO STRENUOUS

Although the Augusta Mine is not quite in the Raggeds Wilderness and the first part of the hike is on a jeep road, hiking up Poverty Gulch to the Augusta Mine is truly enjoyable and the remains of the mine are very interesting. All of the silver mines of the Poverty Gulch area were plagued by massive snowslides in the winter months. An aerial tram was constructed in 1886 to haul ore from the Augusta Mine area to Poverty Gulch, but the following winter it was wrecked by snowslides. In 1908, yet another tram was constructed from the Augusta Mine and once again destroyed by an avalanche which also destroyed the mill below in February of 1909. The tram remains are easy to find near the mine. Most of the mines in this area were no longer worked after 1909, but not before $1,000,000.00 in silver was extracted from them. **NEVER GO IN AN OLD MINE!!!**

Just beyond the beginnings of the old townsite of Pittsburg, the road up Poverty Gulch takes off to the left. If the Slate River is low enough, it is possible to drive a little ways further in a passenger car. However, I will consider this stream crossing to be the trailhead for this hike. After a little more than 1.5 miles, you will come to an intersection with the Daisy Pass Trail which crosses the stream to the left. Some of the Daisy Pass Trail is visible from lower on the Poverty Gulch Road. Be sure to stay right and continue on up into Poverty Gulch, where the deteriorating old road will lead you to the Augusta Mine at 11,000'. As you climb higher, you will have a beautiful view of the Slate River Valley. This is a gorgeous hike to take in the fall as the hillsides wear all their fall colors from the brilliant yellows of the aspens to the reds and oranges of the lower growing foliage.

ANGEL PASS 11,960'
AUGUSTA MOUNTAIN 12,559'
MINERAL POINT 12,506'

USGS Oh-Be-Joyful
TH Poverty Gulch
SE 9200'
TVG 2760' Angel Pass
RT 9 miles
STRENUOUS
TVG 3360' with Augusta Mountain
TVG 3440' with Mineral Point
RT 10.5 with peaks
VERY STRENUOUS

Follow the directions to the Augusta Mine. Hike up the steep slopes to the right of the mine, being careful of a few cliff areas near the mine. Remnants of the old tram cable can occasionally provide a nice handhold on this steep grass and gravel slope. Angel Pass is on the ridge above and slightly to the right. It is easy to become confused as an old trail leading off to the left looks like it goes to an obvious pass. While it does go to an unnamed pass which overlooks Baxter Basin, this is not Angel Pass. The trail to Angel Pass can be picked up higher, joining this old trail from Baxter Basin and leading off to the right. Angel Pass has a spectacular view into Middle Anthracite Creek and Dark Canyon. In the 1880's pack trains of burros carried ore from mines in the Dark Canyon region over Angel Pass and down into Poverty Gulch.

From Angel Pass, it is very easy to climb 12,559', Augusta Mountain by just following the ridge beyond the pass to the summit. If you wish to continue on over to Mineral Point, drop off the ridge after Augusta to avoid some unpleasant terrain on the ridge. To descend from the summit of Mineral Point, go back the way you came until you can see a good scree route down to the upper of the two lakes above the Augusta

Mine, and then follow the drainage down to the mine area. These two lakes are just potholes and do not support fish.

M. A. Tarr, Cyr Pelletier, Fr. Jim Koenigsfeld on Angel Pass
--Photo by Nancy Ruehle

Augusta Mountain and Mineral Point from Angel Pass
--Photo by Nancy Ruehle

AUGUSTA MINE, MTN., ANGEL PASS & MINERAL PT.

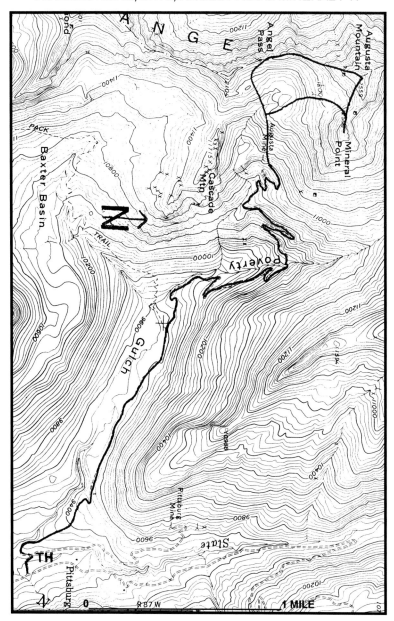

YULE PASS 11,720'
TREASURY MOUNTAIN 13,462'
PURPLE MOUNTAIN 12,958'

USGS Oh-Be-Joyful, Snowmass Mountain
TH Top of Paradise Divide
SE 11,280'
TVG 440' Yule Pass
RT 4 miles
EASY TO MODERATE
TVG 2200' Treasury Mountain
RT 7 miles
MODERATE TO STRENUOUS
TVG 1680' Purple Mountain
RT 6 miles
MODERATE TO STRENUOUS

Yule Pass, at 11,680', is reached by walking 2 miles NW from the summit of Paradise Divide along the flanks of Cinnamon Mountain. This pass, and the creek on its west side, are named for Gunnison pioneer and first sheriff of Gunnison County, George Yule. From the summit of Yule Pass, it is easy to climb 13,462', Treasury Mountain to the north (right) by climbing the ridge on the right directly from Yule Pass and then following the ridge to the summit. This is really a fun ridge to walk. It is also possible to climb this peak by first following the old road leading to some abandoned cement structures which were part of the Eureka Mine tram. It is a much steeper climb beyond the tram. I would recommend going directly from the summit of the pass without following the Eureka Mine road unless you are particularly interested in the old tram.

South of Yule Pass is 12,958', Purple Mountain. To climb this, first go a short ways on the left hand trail on the west side of Yule Pass until it is possible to climb into the basin west of Purple Mountain. After climbing up through the basin to the north ridge of the peak, the ascent of Purple Mountain becomes a moderate and interesting ridge climb. The final scramble up the summit cone is quite steep and loose.

YULE PASS TO MARBLE QUARRIES
USGS Oh-Be-Joyful, Snowmass Mountain, Marble
TH Top of Paradise Divide
SE 11,280'
TVG 400' to Yule Pass
TVG 2000' return to Yule Pass
RT 14 miles
STRENUOUS

Follow the directions to reach the summit of Yule Pass. Take the trail at the summit which leads down into the Yule Creek valley, not the one to the left which contours around the hillside. This trail can be indistinct and occasionally hard to find as you proceed further down into the lower grassy areas of Yule Creek. After about 3.7 miles, the trail will have a fork which is difficult to distinguish because of the willows and water. The trail you want is the right fork and will continue with the main creek. It gradually leads into a canyon, and after a little over a mile, you will be able to look to your left and see the gaping holes of the Yule Quarry. This quarry produced the marble for the Tomb of the Unknown Soldier. Although it is possible to hike down and cross the stream, be aware of private property and obey trespass signs.

The Marble Quarry

YULE PASS, PURPLE & TREASURY MTNS.

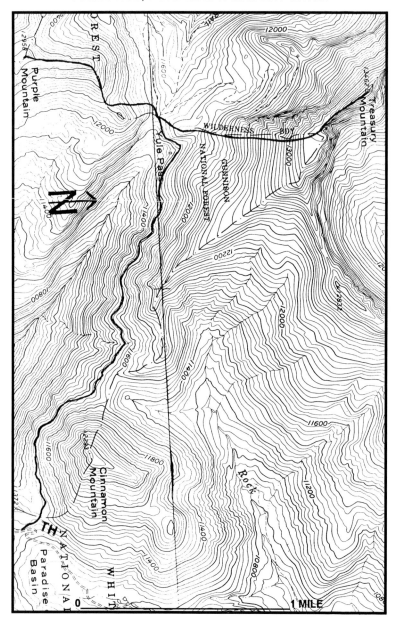

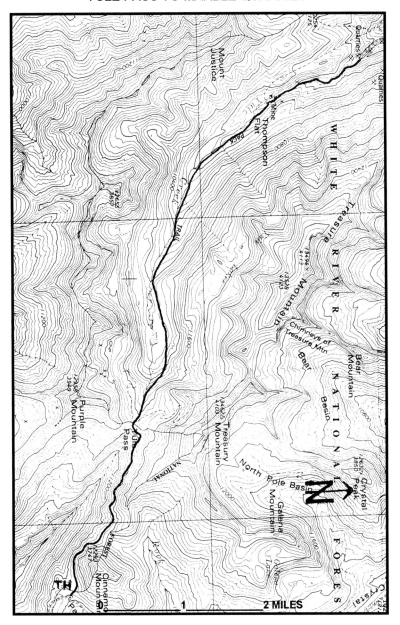

CINNAMON MOUNTAIN 12,293'
USGS Oh-Be-Joyful
TH Top of Paradise Divide
SE 11,280'
TVG 1000'
RT 2 miles
MODERATE

The trailhead for Cinnamon Mountain is at the top of Paradise Divide, just like for the Yule Pass hikes. Although the Yule Pass Trail passes under the face of Cinnamon Mountain, the easiest route for climbing the peak is to head north from the summit of Paradise Divide over to the steep, grassy slopes of the peak which can be seen to the right. Once on these grassy slopes, head in a northwesterly direction to the summit at 12,293'. Even though the route is fairly steep, it is better than trying to climb up scree. The view from the summit is outstanding--Snowmass Mountain, the Maroon Bells, and Pyramid Peak. Return by the same route.

Maroon Bells and Pyramid Peak as seen from Cinnamon Mountain

Snowmass as seen from Cinnamon Mountain

MOUNT BALDY 12,805'
USGS Oh-Be-Joyful
TH Elkton cutoff on Paradise Divide
SE 10,700'
TVG 2100'
RT 5 miles
MODERATE TO STRENUOUS

      On the Slate River Road, drive up the road leading to Paradise Divide. Park your car and begin hiking at about 10,700' where the road from Elkton joins this road. Head NE into the drainage below Baldy and work your way to the ridge. There will be some scree slopes to navigate, but they are not difficult. Once on the ridge, continue to its high point north of you at 12,805'. From the summit, you will be able to see the East River drainage as well as the Slate River drainage. Many people choose Baldy for spring and early summer skiing, but remember the importance of knowing about avalanches for any backcountry snow travel.

      It is also possible to continue driving to the summit of Paradise Divide and then climb the ridge directly towards the east. This ridge will put you on the summit ridge, which can be followed for its entire length to the high point. This is a steeper route than the one described above.

CINNAMON MOUNTAIN & MOUNT BALDY

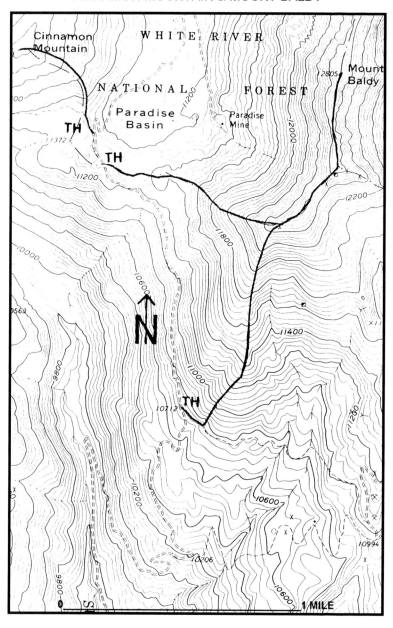

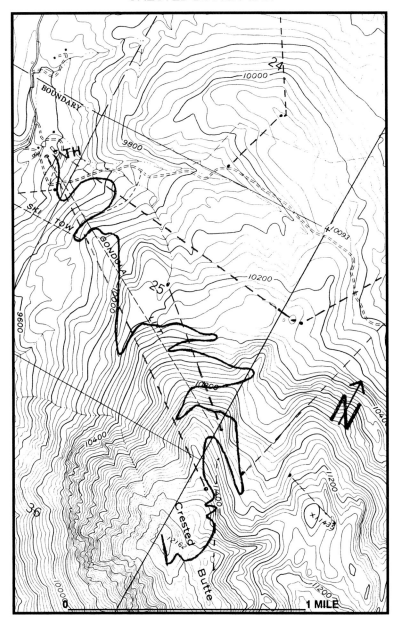

CRESTED BUTTE PEAK 12,162'
USGS Gothic
TH Gothic Building--Crested Butte Mountain Resort
SE 9400'
TVG 2800'
RT 5-8 miles
STRENUOUS

It is always a treasure hunt when hiking at the ski area. Skiers drop things from the lifts as their bulky gloves and mittens pull unobserved items out of pockets, and their skis and other miscellaneous pieces of equipment are lost in seemingly bottomless, deep powder. The service roads used by the grooming equipment in the winter become maintenance roads in the summer. These roads also provide easy access for hiking at the ski area. The road up the front of Crested Butte Ski Area begins to the right of the Gothic Building (Warming House). This road is about 3 miles long and provides a gentle hike to the top of the Silver Queen lift, the one which goes directly up the front of the mountain. There are several fairly steep trails, usually near or right under the lifts, which can be taken between portions of the road to shorten the distance. Since the summit trail leaves from the top of the Silver Queen chairlift, work your way to that point, whether hiking on the road or the little trails.

The summit trail is well-kept, well signed, and alerts hikers of cliff areas. It is important to stay on the trail as there are unexpected dangerous cliffs on this peak which have caused death falls for off-trail hikers. The summit is small and cozy, with views of the entire Crested Butte Valley. Many people choose to buy a ticket at the base area, ride the chairlift to its top, then hike the summit trail and hike down the mountain on the roads or trails. Whatever your choice, it can be a fun place to hike, and you will see many pretty wildflowers on the mountain.

CRESTED BUTTE AREA

Boy Scouts enjoying a break during ski area hike

Gothic Valley as seen from the ski area

JUDD FALLS 9800'
USGS Gothic
TH End of Judd Falls Road
SE 9840'
TVG 100'
RT 2 miles
EASY

From the Judd Falls Trailhead, walk around the vehicle barrier and hike to a sign indicating the trail to Judd Falls and Copper Creek. The overgrown road immediately to the left of this little trail leads to Virginia Basin. The rocky little trail to Judd Falls will take you over a small hump and then drop down to the Copper Creek Trail. You will pass through, or just below, aspen trees, and there are occasional wet areas on the trail, especially during early season. Also, early in the season expect to see lots of Glacier Lilies and Spring Beauties everywhere. Once on the Copper Creek Trail, it is but a few yards down to your right to arrive at the overlook of Judd Falls. At this overlook is a bench placed in memory of Garwood H. Judd, a prominent resident of Gothic who came in 1880 with the silver boom and remained even after the town was essentially deserted. He is referred to as "the man who stayed".

Anne Ash enjoying Judd Falls from the bench

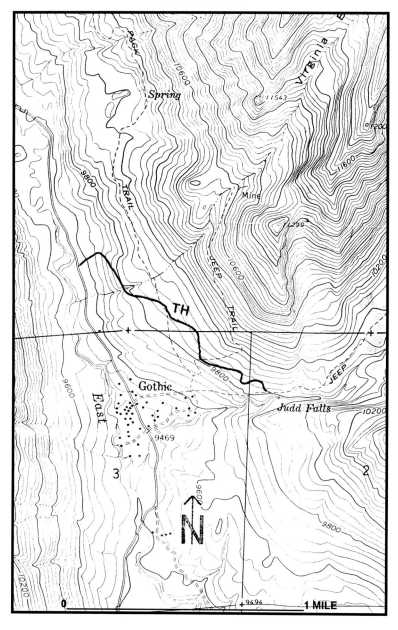

SYLVANITE MINE 11,500'
USGS Gothic
TH End of Judd Falls Road
SE 9840'
TVG 1650'
RT 8 miles
MODERATE

The discovery of balls of silver wires in the Sylvanite Mine brought about a major "boom" in the mining town of Gothic in late 1879 and the early 1880's. **NEVER GO IN AN OLD MINE!!!** Begin at the Judd Falls Trailhead. Follow the directions in the Judd Falls hike to the Copper Creek Trail which winds gently in a northeasterly direction into the Maroon Bells-Snowmass Wilderness.

Boy Scouts outside the Sylvanite Mine

In the early season, the first stream crossing on the Copper Creek Trail, occurring in about 1.5 miles, can be quite high and dangerous with no logs for crossing. Even later in the summer it is a good idea to carry wading shoes for this crossing. Continue following the Copper Creek Trail for approximately 2 more miles and past 2 more stream crossings which probably will have crossing logs, to a junction where a road takes off steeply with an oblique left. Take this road, as it will lead to the Sylvanite Mine. In mid-summer, look for yummy strawberries in the grassy meadows by the road and near the ruins of some old cabins. After arriving at the mine, look across Copper Creek Valley and you can see the trail up Triangle Pass and the big mass of Whiterock Mountain to the right of the pass. Copper Creek supports Colorado River and Snake River Cutthroat for fishing enthusiasts.

COPPER LAKE 11,321'
USGS Gothic, Maroon Bells
TH End of Judd Falls Road
SE 9840'
TVG 1520'
RT 8 miles
MODERATE

Begin at the Judd Falls Trailhead, and follow the directions in the Judd Falls Hike to the Copper Creek drainage and the entrance to the wilderness area. Head NE up the valley on the Copper Creek Trail for about 4 miles. Early in the season all three stream crossings may be quite difficult, with the first being the most dangerous and having no logs. It is a good idea to take a pair of wading shoes any time of the summer. As you near the head of the valley there will be a road to the left which leads to the old Sylvanite Mine. Stay right on the Copper Creek Trail until you come to a junction with Triangle Pass and Copper Lake Trails. Take the Copper Lake Trail for another quarter mile to the lake. Copper Lake is a beautiful place to camp when backpacking. This lake supports Snake River Cutthroat and Rainbow Trout.

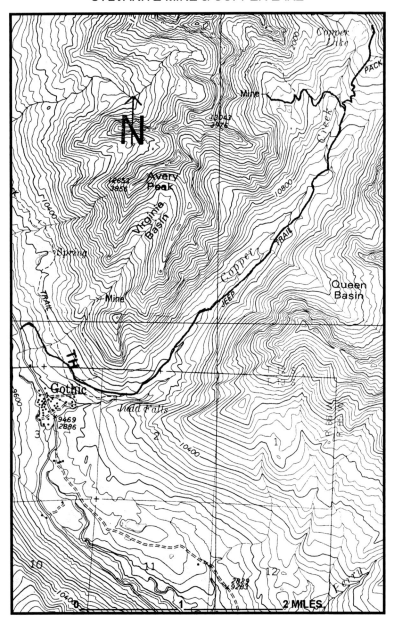

TRIANGLE PASS 12,900'
COPPER PASS 12,580'
EAST MAROON PASS 11,800'

USGS Gothic, Maroon Bells
TH End of Judd Falls Road
SE 9840'
TVG 3100' to Triangle Pass
TVG 60' Triangle Pass to Copper Pass
TVG 520' Copper Pass to East Maroon Pass
RT All three passes 14 miles
VERY STRENUOUS from TH
MODERATE TO STRENUOUS from Copper Lake
RT Triangle Pass 12 miles
STRENUOUS
RT Copper Pass 12 miles
STRENUOUS
RT East Maroon Pass 9.5 miles
MODERATE TO STRENUOUS

Each of these passes can be done separately as a long day hike, or all three can be done together as a backpacking trip with a camp at Copper Lake. The description which follows first is a circle trip which will include all three passes. Follow the directions given in the Copper Lake Hike and camp at the lake.

For the circle tour of the passes the next day, return to the junction with Triangle Pass Trail and hike 2 miles up this new drainage past the north side of Whiterock Mountain to the summit of Triangle Pass. On the way up Triangle Pass, about .5 mile from the summit, notice the trail to Copper Pass which takes off to the left. Continue on to the magnificent view from the summit of Triangle Pass at 12,920'!! For the next part on this circle trip, hike back down from Triangle Pass to the Copper Pass trail and climb the .25 miles to its summit. Here you will have a grand view of Pyramid Peak and the Maroon Bells.

From Copper Pass, follow the trail down into the East Maroon Creek Valley and the intersection with East Maroon Creek Trail at 11,280'. Follow this trail up the north side of East Maroon Pass to its summit at just over 11,800' and then down the other side to Copper Lake.

To climb to the summit of East Maroon Pass only, follow the directions to Copper Lake and continue on the trail to East Maroon Pass. Many people like to hike all the way to Aspen over East Maroon Pass. There is a bus which runs from Maroon Lake Campground into Aspen, and the East Maroon Pass Trail comes out just below the campground.

To climb either Copper Pass or Triangle Pass singly, do not go to Copper Lake, but simply turn right at the trail junction of Triangle Pass and Copper Lake. Follow the directions given above in the circle trip of the passes for either Triangle or Copper Passes.

Nick McCormick on the summit of Copper Pass above East Maroon drainage
--Photo by Sean McCormick

CONUNDRUM HOT SPRINGS 11,200'

USGS Gothic, Maroon Bells
TH End of Judd Falls Road
SE 9840'
TVG 3100' plus 1700' return over pass
RT 15 miles
VERY STRENUOUS from TH or Copper Lake

Follow the directions to Triangle Pass. Hike over Triangle Pass into the Conundrum Creek drainage. About 1.5 miles down this pass is Conundrum Hot Springs where the spring water is 100 degrees F and collected in three small pools. I cannot recommend camping at this fragile and over-used area. The last time I was hiking below the hot springs, I met at least 80 people from the Aspen side going up to camp! Try to visit these hot springs on a daytrip, thus producing far less impact on the area. I suggest camping at Copper Lake. Remember to start your hike very early in the day, as the hot springs lie beneath Electric Peak. Since nudity is the most popular swimwear, you might be running for cover, quite naked, if caught in a thunderstorm! Also remember that the elevation of Triangle Pass is just under 13,000', and you should plan to return across the pass before the afternoon thunderstorms.

Boy Scouts above Conundrum Hot Springs   --Photo by Sean McCormick

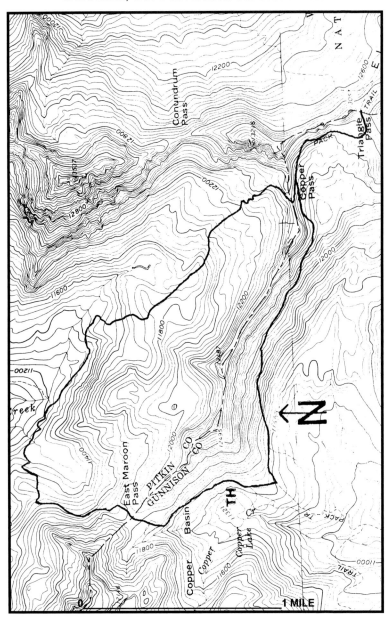

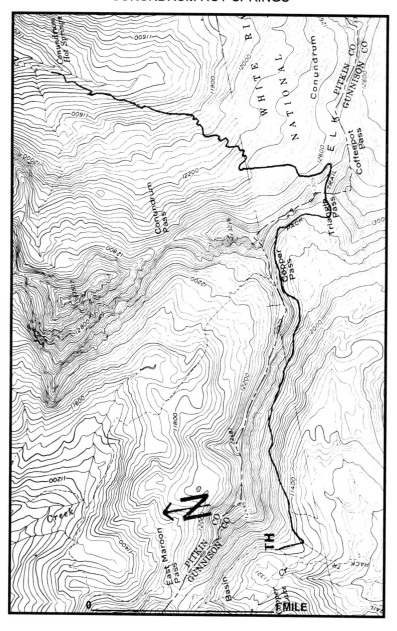

AVERY PEAK   12,653'
USGS Gothic
TH End of Judd Falls Road
SE 9840'
TVG 2850'
RT 6 miles
STRENUOUS

Begin hiking at the parking area at the end of Judd Falls Road, beyond the vehicle barricade. After about one third mile, take the old road on the left. This road is becoming quite overgrown, and is located at the junction with the trail leading to Judd Falls and Copper Creek. The road leads to the Virginia Mine, one of the supporting mines of Gothic during the boom of the mining days. After about 2 miles, the mine will be to your right immediately after a small creek crossing. Just before this creek by the mine, a narrow trail takes off from the road steeply to the right. Follow this trail, which remains quite steep, until the start of Virginia Basin, for the approach to Avery Peak. There is a grand view of Gothic Peak across the valley behind.

Looking from the summit of Avery Peak across to Gothic Mountain

40

At the beginning of Virginia Basin, the trail becomes less steep, continuing on through the timber and further into the basin. When the trail breaks out into the open, continue on for a bit until the trail nears the stream and you can spot a natural place to cross on big flat slabs. From here it is a steep climb up the east facing, grassy slopes to the ridge leading to Avery Peak. Angle north (right) on the way up to the ridge, aiming for the last of the small trees on the ridge. It is a good idea to look back at your route on the way up to avoid getting into loose rock by descending too high in the basin when returning. Once on the ridge, it is then an airy walk to the summit. There are occasional trails on the right which avoid the ridge itself, but care must be taken on loose, crumbly rock. The summit offers a beautiful view of Rustler's Gulch and over towards the Maroon Bells. This hike should only be taken by experienced hikers who don't mind a little exposure.

GOTHIC MOUNTAIN 12,625'
USGS Oh-Be-Joyful
TH Gothic Campground Trail #403
SE 9600'
TVG 3025'
RT 7 miles
STRENUOUS

Climbing Gothic Mountain is easily done from Washington Gulch Trail #403. This trail is also a very popular bicycle route, but only a small portion of the climb of Gothic Mountain is on it. The trail departs from the northern section of the Gothic Campground. Follow the trail through False Hellebore up several switchbacks and into the forest. After about 1.7 miles, the trail will cross Rock Creek. In about .25 mile, the trail will cross some large grassy parks, and at about 10,850', you should leave the trail and head off towards Gothic Mountain on your left. It is possible to pick up a faint trail along the top of a ridge across from the grassy area. Follow this trail through heavy timber until it opens up and goes briefly downhill across an open grassy slope. At the bottom of this grassy slope, either look for a trail or just begin climbing up and mostly south (to your right) until you come out of the timber and can see that you are on the ridge and on your way up Gothic Mountain. Take note of the route you just followed, and especially the location of the ridge you crossed, as they can be elusive on the return trip. Now climb up the ridge ahead to the 12,490', lower summit of Gothic Mountain. There is a good solid path leading to the higher summit at 12,625'. Be sure to start this climb early in the day to avoid afternoon thunderstorms.

CRESTED BUTTE AREA

Looking from the lower to the higher summit of Gothic Mountain

Webelos Scouts on Gothic Mountain with view of Maroon Peak

43

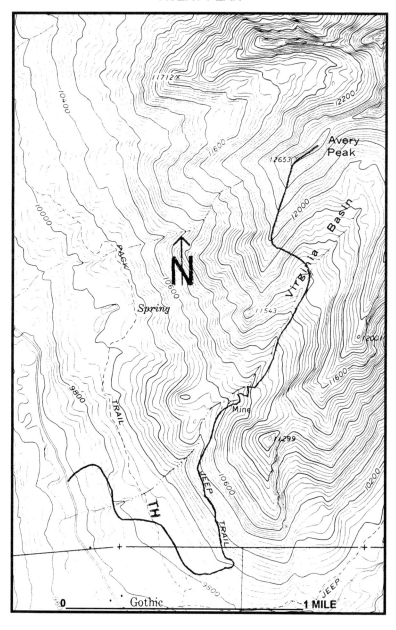

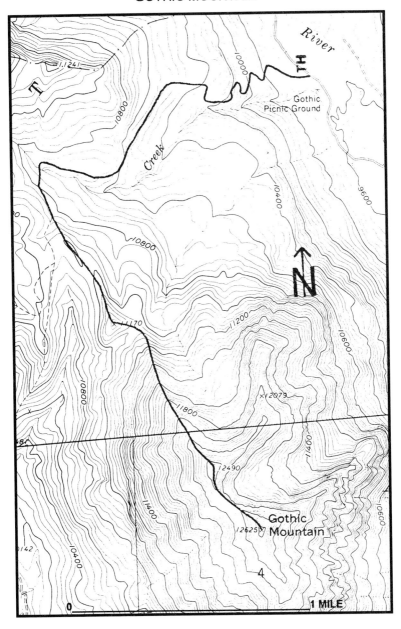

MT. BELLVIEW 12,519'
USGS Snowmass Mountain
TH Gothic Road (FR 317) above Gothic
SE 10,000'
TVG 2500'
RT 3 miles
STRENUOUS

The shortest way to climb Mt. Bellview is to drive up the Gothic Valley along the East River towards Emerald Lake. Park the car at a turnout about 3.5 miles beyond Gothic. The peak is on your right and you only need head in a northeasterly direction up the quite steep, grassy slopes to obtain the ridge. Once on the ridge head NW until you reach the summit of that ridge. Turn right and follow the ridge to the true summit NE of you. From the summit there is a great view of the beautiful Maroon Bells. Looking back the way you came up the ridge gives a view of the ski trails of Crested Butte Mountain Resort. You can also look to see if anyone is on top of Avery Peak across the Rustler's Gulch Valley. Directly across the big East River Valley to the SW is 12,805', Mount Baldy, and to the south is 12,625', Gothic Peak.

Mt. Bellview and avalanche debris from just outside Gothic

A slightly longer, but more gentle route up Bellview is to walk up the Rustler's Gulch Road and then cut over through the forest to reach the first ridge, which is the same ridge which was climbed directly from the Gothic Road. Rustler's Gulch is signed and is about 2.5 miles out of Gothic. Some cars drive a little ways on the Rustler's Gulch road, although Donna Rozman and I spent an extended period of time buried to the axle in an innocuous looking mud puddle which we were attempting to cross in a 4-wheel drive Scout.

View from Mt. Bellview down the Gothic Valley towards Crested Butte Peak

RUSTLER'S GULCH TRAIL

USGS Snowmass Mountain, Maroon Bells, Oh-Be-Joyful
TH Rustler's Gulch turnoff from Gothic Road
SE 9716'
TVG 1360'
RT 8 miles
MODERATE

It is possible to drive a short distance on the Rustler's Gulch Road to find a place to leave your vehicle. An immediate problem as you begin hiking will be the stream crossing. There is a 4-wheel drive road for 1.2 miles to the Wilderness Boundary, and the stream ford on this road is quite deep. My jeep, Nellie, drowned in this ford, but luckily we were able to resuscitate her! To find a shallower crossing, go to the left and up over a small hill to a place where the creek spreads out. Return to the road and continue on it to the gate marking the boundary of the Maroon Bells-Snowmass Wilderness Area. The trail heads north between 12,519', Mt. Bellview on the left and an unnamed 13,010' peak on the right. While still passing along the side of Mt. Bellview, if you look up high on the side, you will be able to see the many switchbacks of the old road leading up to the Silver Spruce Mine.

Continuing on the main trail to the north will bring you to the base of a very steep ridge which joins West Maroon Pass on the other side. The trail will turn east (right) and contour the base of this ridge, culminating in a large cirque topped with Precarious Peak. This is a gentle hike with a beautiful view. After the first stream crossing, there are two more larger crossings which might be a little difficult during high run-off.

Precarious Peak dominates the view at the end of the Rustler's Gulch Trail

13,010' UNNAMED PEAK

USGS Snowmass Mountain, Maroon Bells, Oh-Be-Joyful
TH Rustler's Gulch turnoff from Gothic Road
SE 9716'
TVG 3300'
RT 7.6 miles easy route
RT 5.6 miles steep route
STRENUOUS

Follow the directions to the Wilderness Boundary in the Rustler's Gulch Hike. The easiest, although not the shortest, route to climb this 13,010', Unnamed Peak is to continue on the Rustler's Gulch Trail until you are by the southwest slopes of the long northwest ridge of the peak. Head off the trail up the grassy slopes to reach the end of the ridge, and then follow the ridge to the summit.

The other route to climb this peak is steeper. Before passing through the gate at the Wilderness Boundary, go down to the creek on the right, and find a large log which has fallen across the creek for crossing. Hike up the open meadows and through a small bit of trees to reach the southwest ridge. The ridge is fairly steep and the rock is loose, not so much as to be dangerous, but loose enough to be rather annoying. There is a lot of variation in the type of rock on this ridge.

It's all worth the climb, regardless of the route you choose, when you see the view from this high, tiny summit. Look for the following peaks: Snowmass, Capitol, Maroon, North Maroon, Pyramid, Precarious, Castle, Gothic, Crested Butte, all of the Ruby Range up the Slate River, West Elks, Uncompahgre, Wetterhorn, Stewart, Baldy Chato....

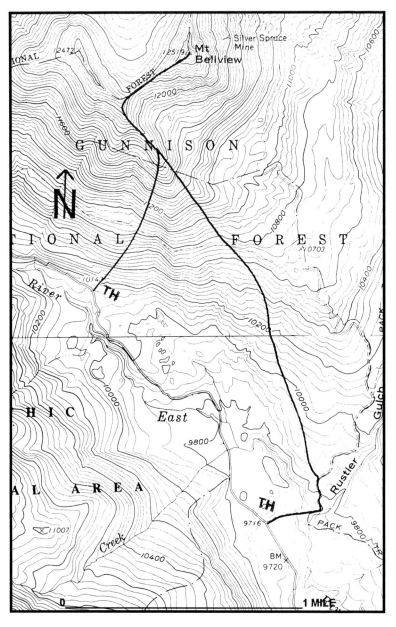

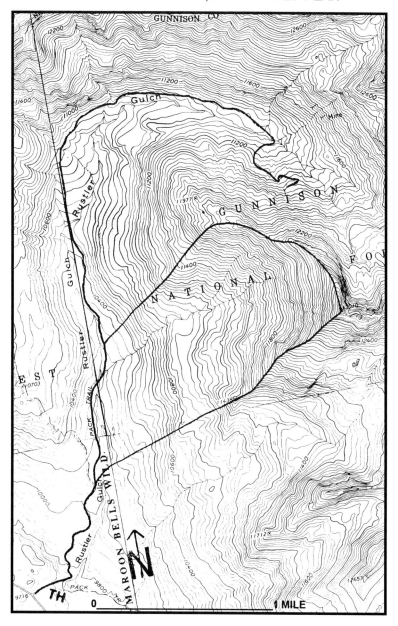

WEST MAROON PASS 12,680'
USGS Snowmass Mountain, Maroon Bells
FRIGID AIR PASS 12,400'
USGS Snowmass Mountain
TH Bottom of the N side of Schofield Pass
SE 10,400'
TVG 2300' to West Maroon Pass
RT 8 miles
TVG 2000' to Frigid Air Pass
RT 8 miles
MODERATE TO STRENUOUS

The start for both Frigid Air and West Maroon Passes is the same. The trailhead is at the bottom of the N side of Schofield Pass, on the right, just after the scary little vehicle bridge. After a few minor switchbacks at the beginning, the first miles leading to either of these passes go through what could only be described as *God's Garden*. Nowhere have I seen wildflowers as lush and plentiful as when hiking this trail up the

Maroon Peak (also called South Maroon Peak)

52

CRESTED BUTTE AREA

East Fork of the Crystal River. In July, I know I must have seen almost every kind of wildflower, with especially gorgeous clumps of Colorado Columbine. This valley appears to be covered with a multicolored crazyquilt. In August the landscape is dominated by pinks and purples of Rosy Paintbrush and various composites, interspersed with yellow sunflowers. In a good snow year, this is a hike that should not be missed.

After a little less than 3 miles of gentle hiking, the trail splits, and the right fork climbs steeply up to the top of West Maroon Pass and a glorious view of Pyramid Peak and South Maroon Peak. Of particular notice near the summit of West Maroon Pass are several clumps of Purple Leaf Groundsel, a pretty plant with purple leaves and a yellow blossom, growing in the maroon-colored gravel. The Western Fringed Gentian, with fringed petals which twist when they close, are also especially prolific on the upper approach to the pass.

Back down at the junction of the West Maroon and Frigid Air Trails, the left fork of the trail skirts back along the side of Belleview Mountain and then climbs steep switchbacks to the summit of Frigid Air Pass. This pass overlooks the stunning, pink and green, Fravert Basin, and provides a beautiful, closeup view of the Maroon Bells.

Pyramid Peak

53

FRIGID AIR PASS & WEST MAROON PASS

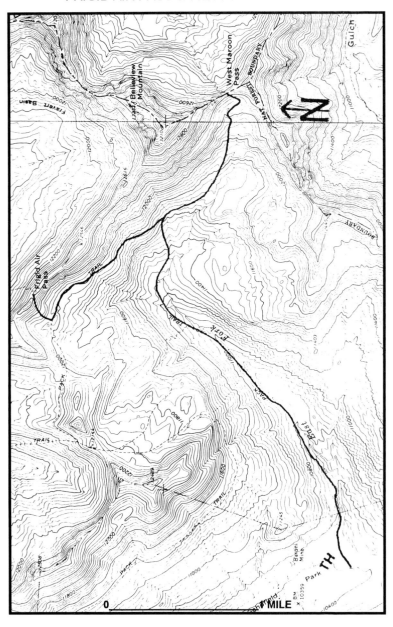

TOUR OF THE BELLS

USGS Snowmass Mountain, Maroon Bells
TH Bottom of the N side of Schofield Pass
SE 10,400'
DAY 1 MODERATE TO STRENUOUS
TVG 2300' (6.5 miles)
DAY 2 STRENUOUS
TVG 2300' (7 miles)
DAY 3 MODERATE TO STRENUOUS
TVG 2000' (6 miles)
DAY 4 MODERATE
TVG 1400' (6 miles)
RT 25.5 miles

Beginning at the trailhead at the foot of Schofield Pass, hike up the East Fork Creek, always taking the trail marked to West Maroon Pass. After a little less than 3 miles of the most gorgeous wildflowers, you will come to a trail intersection with Frigid Air Pass heading NW (left) and West Maroon Pass continuing on to the SE (right). Continue on the West Maroon Pass Trail which now climbs steeply up to the summit at about 12,700'. After enjoying the spectacular view, leave the summit to drop rapidly into the West Maroon Creek drainage on the other side. After another 2.5 miles, nice campsites can be found in the trees near the second of 2 larger stream crossings.

The summer of 1995, which finally began about mid-July, was particularly unusual at West Maroon Pass. On July 15, the valley leading to the pass was still carpeted with Glacier Lilies and Spring Beauties. The pass itself was totally snowed in. While on a Boy Scout hike on July 28, I found the east side of the pass was still totally snowed in, and the last part of the west side wasn't much different. On the west side, there were a few Colorado Columbine starting to bloom in odd places, like under the willows, and that was about all the flowers. Then during an early September backpacking trip, I found there were still some residual snowbanks on the east side of the pass and the ground was covered with Snow Buttercups. The west side of the pass had flowers typical of late July, and, in addition, all of the August and September flowers were blooming. It's pretty amazing to be able to see the whole spectrum of the wildflowers that bloom in an area all in the same hike!

M. A. Tarr on top of Buckskin Pass with Pyramid Peak in background
--Photo by John Tarr

On the second day, continue down the trail for about 1.5 miles past Crater Lake to the intersection with the Buckskin Pass Trail. As you near Crater Lake and are passing in between the Maroon Bells and Pyramid Peak, the classic picture of the Bells will begin to evolve on your left. All the way up 12,462', Buckskin Pass, there will be a beautiful, changing view of Pyramid Peak behind you. At the top of the pass is a splendid view of Snowmass and Hagerman Peaks, and Snowmass Mountain, distinguished by its prominent snowfield. On the way up Buckskin Pass, it is possible to drop packs and take a side trip to Willow Pass which is just north of Buckskin Pass. After descending Buckskin Pass, continue on to Snowmass Lake for camping.

CRESTED BUTTE AREA

The third day of the trip begins by contouring around Snowmass Lake and then winding up beneath Snowmass Peak to 12,400', Trail Rider Pass. On the descent of Trail Rider Pass, you will hike through a beautiful high meadow and then down into the North Fork Valley above Lead King Basin. There will be a trail intersection with a marker directing you east into this valley and away from Geneva Lake. Traveling up the North Fork Valley is very remote and you will be greeted with a gorgeous waterfall at the beginning of the climb up into Fravert Basin. You may choose to either camp below, or up at the beginning of the basin. Fravert Basin is dominated by Maroon Peak on the east side, and the basin can only be described as being pink and green.

View of Snowmass Lake from the trail up to Trailrider Pass

CRESTED BUTTE AREA

On the last day of your *Tour of the Bells,* continue through the lush alpine meadows of Fravert Basin and up to 12,400', Frigid Air Pass. After the immediate descent of the pass, you will contour around the base of Belleview Mountain to the intersection with West Maroon Pass. From this intersection, it is all downhill back to the trailhead from which you started. While out on this tour, you will have completely circled the Maroon Bells, as well as viewed Pyramid Peak, and Snowmass Mountain, all of which are 14,000' peaks.

The Maroon Bells reflected in Maroon Lake

TOUR OF THE BELLS -- DAY 1

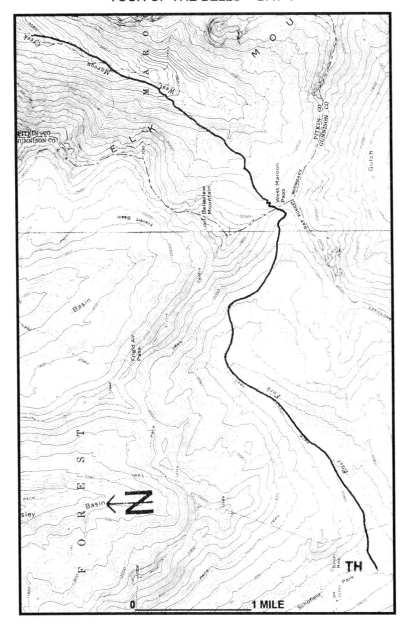

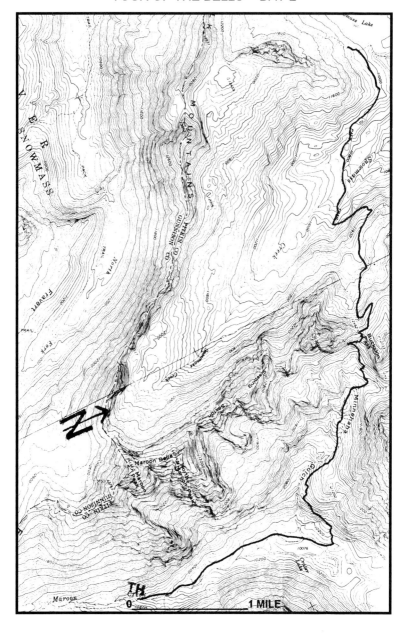

TOUR OF THE BELLS -- DAY 3

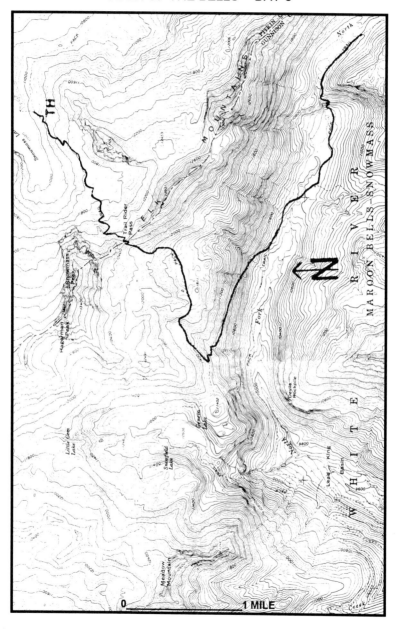

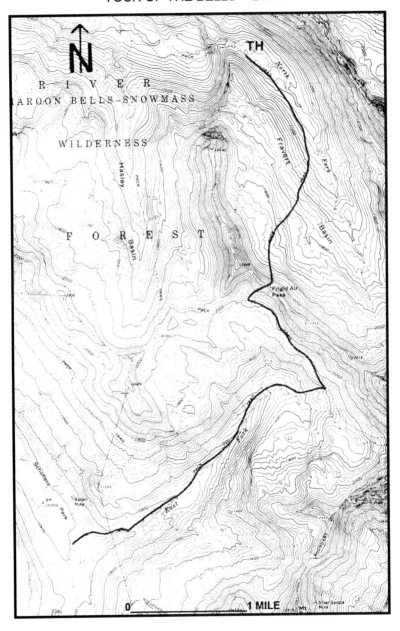

OHIO CREEK VALLEY

Although parts of the beautiful, eighteen mile long, Ohio Creek Valley which lies NW of Gunnison, have been sold to developers, much of it continues to be ranching country. The earlier history of this valley saw very active coal mining, as well as ranching. Driving up this valley from Highway 135, the two most outstanding features are the rock formation known as the Castles on the left and Carbon Peak on the right. During the summer, the roadside is flanked by colorful Larkspur and Scarlet Gilia, highlighted with assorted yellow composite flowers. In the fall, the Ohio Creek Valley can't be beat for enjoying the brilliant yellow and occasional red of the aspen trees. To reach this valley, drive 3 miles north from the last stoplight in Gunnison on Highway 135 and turn left onto CR 730. The Ohio Creek Road (CR 730) goes over Ohio Pass and intersects the Kebler Pass Road which goes east to Crested Butte or west over Kebler Pass.

Trailheads and roads turning off Ohio Creek Road are the following distances from Highway 135:

Mill Creek Road (CR 727) is 9 miles
Mill Creek TH is 13.5 miles
Swampy Pass TH is 18.4 miles
Base of Ohio Pass is 18.4 miles
Beaver Ponds TH is 19.3 miles
Ohio Pass Railroad Grade is 20.8 miles
Summit of Ohio Pass is 22.2 miles
Kebler Pass Road (CR 12) is 23.5 miles
Crested Butte is 31.5 miles

MILL CREEK TRAIL
USGS Squirrel Creek
TH Ohio Creek Road
SE 9000'
TVG 300'
RT 2.5 miles
EASY

It is so easy to create a fantasy about the castles high in the mountains above Mill Creek as you see them come into view on the drive up Ohio Creek Valley. Thinking about castles leads to fairy tales, and this can set the scene for a nice walk with children up Mill Creek with its pretty spires. After driving approximately 4.5 miles on the Mill Creek Road (CR 727), park in the open meadow just below the wilderness boundary and then walk beyond the boundary along the hillside next to the Eilebrecht Ditch. The beginning of this trail differs from the one shown on the USGS map because the trail has been rerouted to the south side of the creek to avoid private property. There is a short, steep uphill where the trail skirts above a major washout that occurred a number of years ago. After the trail goes down to the stream and through a crossing, it joins the original trail shown on the USGS map. You can spot the original trail across the creek to help find the crossing. This crossing area is in a wide open meadow and a lovely place to picnic unless, of course, the cows have chosen to picnic there, also. The beautiful spires are intermittently visible during the hike to the stream crossing, and exquisite when the terrain opens up into meadow at the stream. For trout fishing, Mill Creek supports Rainbow, Brown, Brook and Cutthroat.

STORM PASS 12,460'
WEST ELK PEAK 13,035'

USGS Squirrel Creek, West Elk Peak
TH Ohio Creek Road
SE 9000'
DAY 1 MODERATE TO STRENUOUS
TVG 2800' (6.5 miles)
DAY 2 MODERATE
TVG 1235' to West Elk Peak (6 miles)
DAY 3 EASY TO MODERATE
TVG 0 (6.5 miles)
RT 16 miles Storm Pass
RT 19 miles with peak

This is one of the most beautiful hikes in the West Elk Wilderness. Considering the eight miles to Storm Pass you might wish to make this hike into a 2-day backpack trip, and there are beautiful campsites on the way. The surrounding terrain is very rugged and wild. Follow the directions as described in the Mill Creek Hike to the stream crossing. After the crossing, the hike will remain gentle for awhile, and then climb quite steeply up several switchbacks which will take you from about 10,400' to 11,200'. After the switchbacks, the trail will again remain fairly mellow until the base of Storm Pass, climbing up just a bit to the intersection with the North Baldy Trail. After a big snow winter, you will be able to see evidence of the many avalanches by the remaining debris until late into the summer, and in early summer you might expect to lose the trail under snow. If camping, begin looking for your campsite before leaving the trees and before the intersection with North Baldy Trail.

After the intersection with the North Baldy Trail, the terrain will change from steep walls, spires and waterfalls to more open tundra. From the top of 12,440', Storm Pass, there is a beautiful view of the Castles to the north. To climb 13,035', West Elk Peak, head west from the summit of Storm Pass to the unnamed subpeak which is at 12,968'. My husband has named this peak, Goat Peak, as our son, Ben, was surprised when he awakened from a short nap on the summit and found himself face to face with a Mountain Goat. Ben uttered an expletive, after which the goat responded with one of his own, and then quickly jumped off the summit.

Go up and over the summit of the subpeak, drop to the saddle at 12,720', and then follow the grassy ridge up to the rounded summit of West Elk Peak. The view from West Elk Peak, the highest point around, seems to dwarf the surrounding peaks across the valley. Return via the same route.

The Castles & Ohio Creek Valley from West Elk Peak --Photo by John Tarr

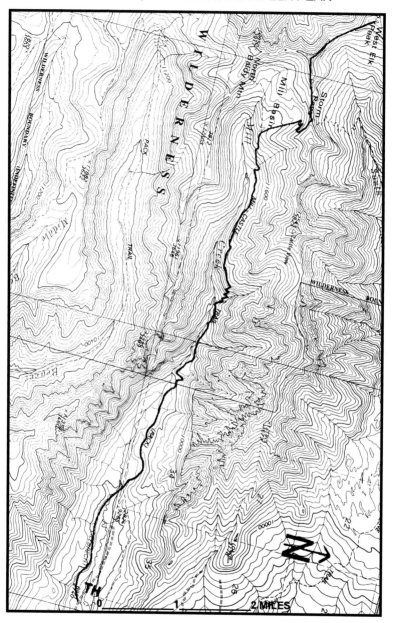

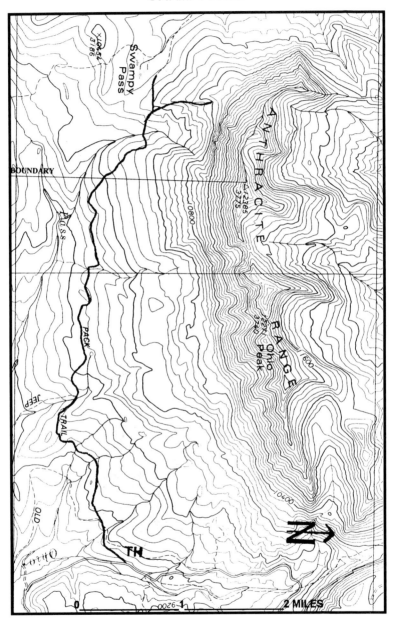

SWAMPY PASS 10,400'
USGS Mt Axtell, Anthracite Range
TH Bottom of Ohio Pass
SE 8980'
TVG 1420'
RT 9.5 miles
MODERATE

About 3/4 of the trail to Swampy Pass is bordered on the north by the West Elk Wilderness, but not included in it. It is, however, closed to motorized vehicles. Up until the wilderness boundary, you might encounter some mountain bikes, although I think it is more likely that you will encounter horses. If the name, *Swampy Pass*, doesn't hint at this, I would recommend that if you have new hiking boots and wish to keep them looking new, don't select this trail. There are lots of stream crossings and muddy areas on the Swampy Pass Trail, but, regardless, this trail is very beautiful. The first portion of the trail enters and winds through lovely aspen, and these first couple of miles can't be beat for an aspen walk in the fall, as well as beautiful wildflowers in the summer. On an early summer hike I saw Western Yellow Violets, Ballheaded Waterleaf, Bluebells, Glacier Lilies and Western Spring Beauties, just to name a few.

The Anthracite Range from the side of Carbon Peak

OHIO CREEK VALLEY

After 3 larger stream crossings, together with multiple smaller stream crossings, you will come to a lovely open area and the first major fork in the trail at the intersection with the Pass Creek Trail. Keep right to remain on Swampy Pass Trail as the sign indicates. Shortly after this sign are gorgeous views of the castles on the left and the Anthracites on the right. After the open area, you will pass a swamp and then again enter the forest, gradually changing from aspen to spruce and fir. The last portion of the trail is in a deep forest until the final larger stream crossing in another large open area, above which and to the left, is 10,409', Swampy Pass.

Actually, the view from the summit of the pass is mediocre compared to what you can see if you stay near the Anthracites and climb up a ridge forming the head of the basin at the west end of the Anthracite Range. This extra 200 vertical feet allows a full view of the Castles and West Elks, the entire Ohio Creek Valley and the great expanse at the west end of the Anthracite Range.

The Castles from the head of the basin above Swampy Pass

OHIO PASS RAILROAD GRADE
USGS Mt. Axtell
TH Ohio Pass Road
SE 9520'
TVG 100'
RT 2 miles
EASY

This trail follows a portion of the old railroad grade which was constructed by the Denver and South Park Railroad in late 1881 and early 1882 in an effort to join Baldwin and Ruby-Irwin via Ohio Pass. Although much of the grade was constructed, the company abandoned the project in March 1882 and it was never used. As you approach the bottom of Ohio Pass, near the 18 mile marker just before the Swampy Pass Trailhead, look up to the high slope ahead to see the rock work that went into shoring up this intended railroad grade. Continue driving up Ohio Pass 2.4 miles past the Swampy Pass Trailhead to a road which takes off to the right. This will be the third road to the right after Swampy Pass Trailhead. It is possible to drive your car a few hundred yards down this road to a place to turn around, although the road may be obstructed by a huge mudhole.

The small road leading to the Ohio Pass RR Grade from the Ohio Pass Road

71

OHIO CREEK VALLEY

The destination for this hike only involves approximately the first mile of the trail to the location where the railroad company had planned a loop (switchback) for the train. You will be hiking on the lower portion of the railroad grade, below the upper rockwork that was visible earlier. This is a wonderful trail for children because of the gentle grade, and at the loop, you are able to see how huge rocks were placed to make a culvert which would have allowed the stream to pass under the train.

The grassy knoll which leads to the RR culverts

Early in the hike, you will cross two large talus slopes, after which the trail turns into a single track. After crossing two more short talus areas, watch on the right for a large, grassy knoll, the top of which joins the trail. Leave the main trail and follow along the top of the first knoll, taking a vague trail down and then back up a couple of steep embankments as you start around the loop of the switchback. If you miss the first knoll, there will be another one shortly, and they are separated by a large pool of water. Notice that this water which is pooled on one side, passes under the hillside and then rushes out into a stream. It has passed through a rock culvert underneath. There is another functioning culvert at the back of the loop where a drainage from Carbon Peak enters the main tributary of Ohio Creek. Further around on the loop, there is an unfinished culvert. This last culvert is the most interesting one since it was never covered, thus providing the opportunity to see how these culverts were made. It is so impressive that these rock culverts, constructed by hand, continue to function 113 years later.

There are Rainbow and Brook Trout in the creek near the trail. On the return walk enjoy the beautiful view of the castles across Ohio Creek Valley. This trail has some minor use by locals on mountain bikes or motorcycles.

CARBON PEAK 12,079'
USGS Mt. Axtell
TH Ohio Pass Road
SE 9520'
TVG 2560'
RT 8 miles
STRENUOUS

Hike on the old railroad grade to the middle of the loop described in the Ohio Pass Railroad Grade Hike. Here you will see a drainage entering Ohio Creek, via the underground railroad culvert. As you face up this drainage, a short, steep, rocky trail will be on your right and leads to the top of the ridge. Take this trail and continue hiking along the top of this ridge on a vague trail which is quite easy to follow on the top of the ridge. In just under a mile you will come to an intersection with the old Carbon Peak Trail which is marked by a cairn.

The old trail is not particularly well-defined either, although it is wider and a bit more distinct. Follow this new trail as it continues up the drainage, which becomes dry, dark and filled with fallen trees. Keep going. There will be more cairns beyond this dark area as the trail climbs up the west side of the peak. There are some trees most of the way to the summit ridge, although the forest becomes less dense. Carbon Peak, at 12,079', has a gorgeous summit, which drops into a huge cirque on the northeast and several avalanche chutes on the east and south.

Fr. Jim Koenigsfeld on the summit of Carbon Peak with Whetstone Mountain (r) and Crested Butte Peak (l) in the background

I recommend using the route which I have described, rather than trying to find the beginning of the old trail that's shown on the USGS map. The original stream crossing no longer exists, the new one is hard to find, and the lower portion of the trail is quite overgrown and indistinct. The route from the old railroad grade intersects and follows the better portion of the old trail and, thanks to the Denver and South Park Railroad, there is a culvert for the stream crossing.

MT. AXTELL 12,055'
USGS Mt. Axtell
TH Ohio Pass Road
SE 9520'
TVG 2530'
RT 8 miles
STRENUOUS

V. F. Axtell was a lumberman during the early days near Crested Butte. He cut timber for his sawmill from Mt. Axtell, and the mountain was named in his honor. Axtell was the great grandfather of Gunnison native, Clinton S. Spencer.

V. F. Axtell in his Conveyance Office in Crested Butte in 1896
Photo courtesy of C. S. Spencer

To climb Mt. Axtell, hike for 2.3 miles on the gentle trail of the old railroad grade beyond the old railroad loop and through a larger stream crossing. When you come to a huge talus slope on the left which appears to go all the way to the top of a peak, head north, either up this talus or the open grassy slopes beside it. Head for the visible summit, although you will discover that it is a false summit on your ascent of 12,055', Mt. Axtell. Continue climbing up until you reach the southeast end of a long summit ridge. The view as you climb along this summit ridge is outstanding, as the northeast face of Mt. Axtell is very steep. Once on the summit you can look down on Green Lake which is nestled up against this steep face. Do not underestimate this climb, as essentially all of the elevation gain occurs when you start up the peak, not on the approach.

Walking along the summit ridge of Mt. Axtell

WHETSTONE MOUNTAIN 12,516'
USGS Mt. Axtell, Crested Butte
TH Ohio Pass Road
SE 9520'
TVG 3000'
RT 12 miles
STRENUOUS

This is a long, but gorgeous approach to one of the most magnificent peaks in the Gunnison Valley. This is the peak which is southwest (left) of Highway 135 just before the town of Crested Butte. At the writing of this book, there is no easement through private property from Highway 135 to allow the climb of Whetstone Mountain by a shorter approach. Check with the local U. S. Forest Service Office to see if that has changed. The longer approach from the back side of the peak which will be described here is, however, not difficult, and there are beautiful places to camp right up at the base of the peak.

This approach to Whetstone is on the same gentle trail as that used for the Ohio Pass Railroad, Carbon Peak and Mt. Axtell, and it is just under 5 miles. There are three larger stream crossings, but none are difficult or very deep. Two trails from the east side of Carbon Peak join this main trail on the right at about 9600' and then again at around 10,000'. There are many chances to see Whetstone as you walk up the valley, and you have opportunity to plan your route to the summit. Near the end of the approach, the trail will be quite muddy and close to a stream as you climb upwards. After this wet area at about 10,600', you will come out into a flatter, open area. At this point, the willows, not the trail, will branch, with the left branch remaining beside the trail, and the other branch growing up a small drainage to the right. Here you can head straight through the timber to the base of your climb, or follow the right branch of willows for a short distance to gain a better view of your route before heading through the timber. Either way, it is but a short walk through the timber.

The route up the last 2000' vertical feet will be obvious as soon as you come out into the open. There are many fine places to camp in the trees, not far from water. The view from the summit of Whetstone Mountain is grand as you look down on the town of Crested Butte, across to the Elk Mountains, and back to Carbon Peak, Mt. Axtell, and the West Elks.

Carbon Peak from summit of Whetstone Mountain

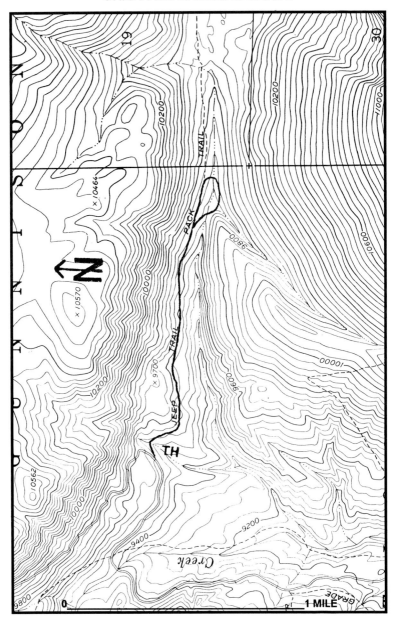

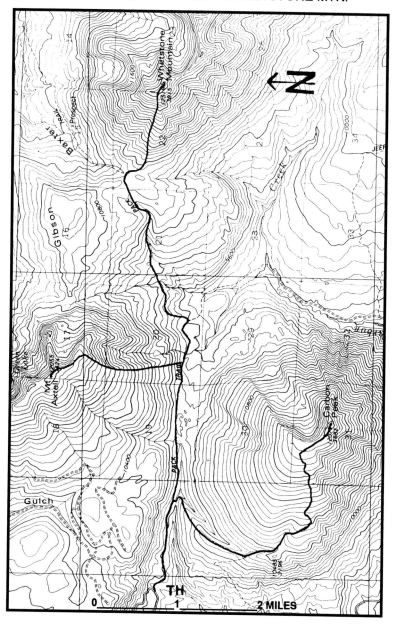

BEAVER PONDS
USGS Mt Axtell
TH Ohio Pass Road
SE 9,330'
TVG 200'
RT 1 mile
EASY TO MODERATE

The Beaver Ponds on Ohio Pass are just inside the West Elk Wilderness. Although this site once contained an improved picnic site, it is returning to its natural state due to the wilderness designation. The hike is an easy .5 mile to the Beaver Ponds and passes through lovely aspen groves. The trail is also flanked on both sides by waist-high foliage with abundant Cow Parsnips and ferns. The Beaver Ponds are a great place to take children for hiking, fishing for Brook Trout and a picnic in a beautiful setting just below the Anthracites.

Trail through the aspens to the Beaver Ponds

OHIO PASS FALLS
USGS Mt. Axtell
TH Top of Ohio Pass
SE 10,000'
TVG 200'
RT 2 miles
EASY TO MODERATE

This beautiful falls is visible from the Ohio Pass Road as you are nearing the summit of Ohio Pass, approximately 3 miles from the Swampy Pass Trailhead. From the car, try to spot the trail leading to the falls. Find the talus slope and you should be able to trace the trail to its start next to an old jeep road. After spotting the trail, continue driving another .8 miles to the summit of Ohio Pass.

The old jeep road begins at the left of the summit marker of the pass. Hike on this old road for .6 miles until you see the first small talus slope, intermixed with trees. It can be difficult to find the beginning of the trail, but once located, it is relatively easy to follow all the way to the waterfall. The start of the trail is on the lower edge of these first rocks, goes about 50 feet on rocks, and then immediately enters the low evergreens.

Ohio Pass Falls from the Ohio Pass Road

Although this trail is short, the second half climbs across steep open slopes. In early summer, the entire hillside is filled with Western Pasqueflowers. Take care on the rotten and slippery rock near the edges of the falls.

OHIO PEAK 12,271'
USGS Mt. Axtell
TH Top of Ohio Pass
SE 10,000'
TVG 2270'
RT 5 miles
MODERATE TO STRENUOUS

It is easiest to climb Ohio Peak by following the trail to the top of the Ohio Pass Waterfall. After this, continue following the trail, when you can find it, onwards and upwards into the big basin above the waterfall. Work your way up to the top of this basin by bearing slightly to the right. Once above the basin, follow along the top (south) to the left and aim for the saddle ahead. Ohio Peak will be the first high point on the west (right) and it is a nice ridge walk up to the summit. Ohio Peak is not the highest peak in the Anthracite Range as there are two higher peaks further west. The wildflowers on this peak are beautiful, and the view from the top is outstanding.

Anthracites from the summit of Ohio Peak with East Beckwith Mtn beyond

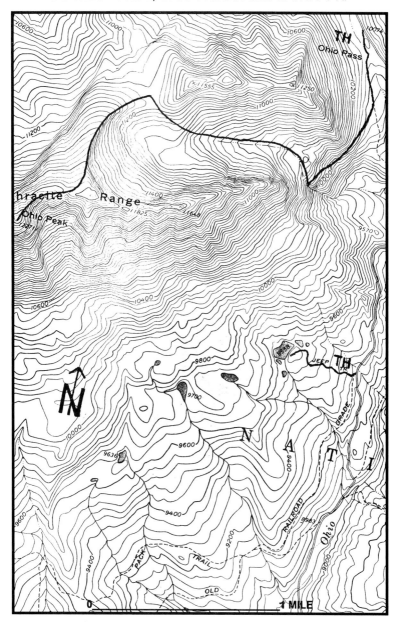

CURECANTI AND THE WEST ELKS

The Curecanti National Recreation Area was named for the Ute War Chief, Curecante, who participated in treaty negotiations in Washington. The hikes of the Curecanti are west of Gunnison, just before Blue Mesa Reservoir and further downstream by the Morrow Point Reservoir. The three huge dams built on the Gunnison River, creating Blue Mesa Reservoir, Morrow Point Reservoir, and Crystal Reservoir, were all part of the Curecanti Project which was begun in 1962. The purpose of the dams is to supply irrigation water and hydroelectric power. All three dams were completed by 1977.

The trailheads for Curecanti hikes and the West Elk Wilderness leaving from Highway 50 (west) are the following distances from the last stoplight on the west side of Gunnison:

Neversink TH is 5 miles
Rainbow Lake Road is 13.8 miles
Dillon Pinnacles TH is 20.3 miles
Blue Mesa Dam (Highway 92) is 25.7 miles
    Soap Creek Road (721 RD) is 1.5 miles
        Soap Creek Campground is 8.7 miles
    Pioneer Point/Curecanti Creek TH is 5.8 miles
    Hermit's Rest TH is 17 miles
    Crystal Creek TH is 24 miles
Pine Creek TH is 26.9 miles

NEVERSINK TRAIL
USGS McIntosh Mountain
TH Neversink, Highway 50
SE 7600'
TVG 0
RT 1.5 miles
EASY

Located off Highway 50 at the Neversink Fishing and Picnic Area, this little trail wanders placidly next to the Gunnison River, through cottonwoods, willows and Wild Rose bushes. It is the perfect place for a gentle, quiet walk with children and an ideal place to look for birds and other possible wildlife. There are benches along the way, as well as numerous little trails leading to the river's edge. The close proximity of the river and the existence of small creek bridges without siderails, necessitate that small children be constantly supervised. The Gunnison River has changed its course in this area during the high waters of both 1993 and 1995.

Cole Thompson on the Neversink Trail

NEVERSINK TRAIL

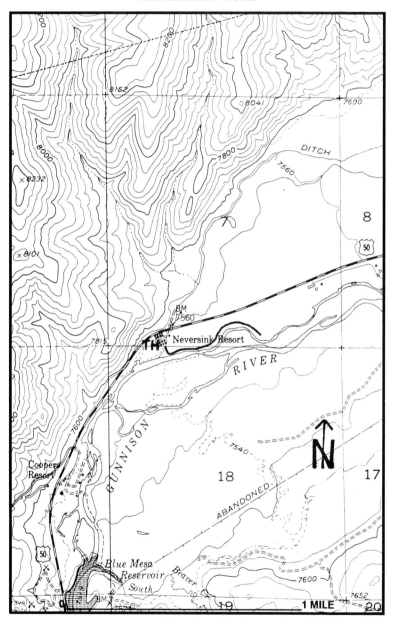

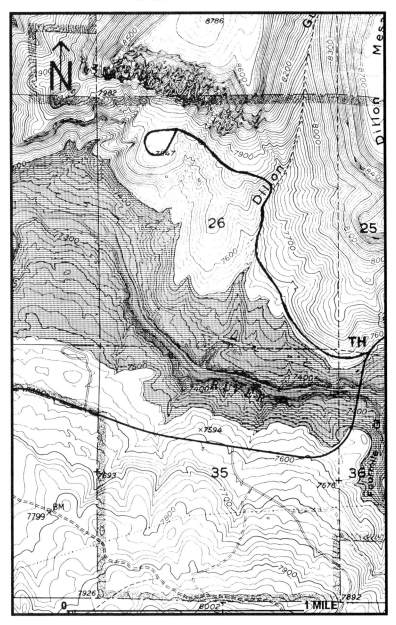

DILLON PINNACLES
USGS Sapinero
TH Highway 50 west
SE 7400'
TVG 450'
RT 4 miles
EASY TO MODERATE

      The Dillon Pinnacles Trail begins at the pullout just before the main bridge spanning the west end of Blue Mesa Reservoir. Begin by walking a short way on the pavement ramp until you see the trail taking off to the right. The trail will parallel the lake for a while and then turn up the hill towards the pinnacles. There are several resting benches and informative signs describing the geological and volcanic history of the pinnacles. At the end of the trail just below these sharp pinnacles, is a loop which goes over for a great view of the lake. This is a very gentle hike and suitable for most ages. From April to July is tick season in the Gunnison Valley, and this particular area has lots of ticks, so be sure to check for them after your hike. Try this hike by moonlight.

The Dillon Pinnacles --Photo by Nancy Vogel

PINE CREEK TRAIL
USGS Sapinero
TH Highway 50 west
SE 7600'
TVG 400' on return
RT 2 miles
EASY TO MODERATE

Unlike the Curecanti Creek and Hermit's Rest Trails, the Pine Creek Trail descends to the Gunnison River on the south side of the canyon along Pine Creek. The initial descent is 180' vertical on 232 steps. Once at the river level, the trail follows the old grade of the Denver and Rio Grande Railroad. There are interpretive signs which tell the incredible story of this narrow gauge railroad. This trail is also the access to the Morrow Point Boat Tours and parking space is limited at the trailhead.

CURECANTI CREEK TRAIL
USGS Curecanti Needle
TH Pioneer Point, Highway 92
SE 8033'
TVG 880" on return
RT 4 miles
MODERATE

Curecanti Creek Trail leaves from the parking area at Pioneer Point on Highway 92. Follow the trail around behind the outhouse to a sign describing the trail. At the sign, the right fork leads onto the trail, while the left fork leads to an overlook for a view of the Morrow Point Reservoir and the end of the trail far below. The upper portion of the trail is in sagebrush and scrub oak (red in the fall). Not far from the start of the trail I saw a blooming Monument Plant, which was quite unusual as they don't bloom very often. Initially the trail contours around below the highway before beginning the major descent into the canyon via well-maintained switchbacks.

The top of the canyon from Pioneer Point

During the walk down by Curecanti Creek, you may feel like you are in the tropics with all the lush vegetation growing at the base of steep granite walls of the canyon. The trail is flanked by Wild Roses and raspberries. The rocks are covered with thick mosses, and I saw a beautiful patch of Spotted Saxifage hanging onto some huge boulders. Of special interest also, were several 3 foot high plants of Many-flowered Stickseed, with the pretty little pale blue forget-me-not flowers at the top. During run-off, Curecanti Creek will be a roily tumble of water, spilling down its own little canyon to enter the Gunnison River, now backed up into the Morrow Point Reservoir. After the second bridge crossing of Curecanti Creek, you will arrive at a picnic/fishing spot, complete with a picnic table, outhouse and even a beach. Curecanti Creek supports Rainbow, Brown and Brook Trout for some good fishing.

The area at the end of the trail is across from the famous Curecanti Needle. This is the rock formation which was used in the advertisements for the Denver and Rio Grande Railroad when it ran through the treacherous Black Canyon. William Jackson Palmer and his railroad men began construction of the railroad through the canyon in the summer of 1881 and finished in the summer of 1882. Many railroaders lost their lives in the Black Canyon due to avalanches and rock slides until the Rio Grande left the Gunnison Country for good in 1954. It is well worth your time to walk over to the overlook at the top of the trail to gain some appreciation for the full magnitude of this railroading history.

HERMIT'S REST

USGS Cimarron
TH Highway 92
SE 8973'
TVG 1800' on return
RT 6 miles
MODERATE

Scrub oak and pine, together with a few juniper and other conifer trees, border the 3 mile trail down to the Morrow

Point Reservoir. As with most of the trails in the Curecanti National Recreation Area, the trail is well-maintained and dotted with resting benches along the way. Small pieces of mica, glistening in the sun, add to the beauty of this trail. During most of the hike it is possible to see the reservoir, as well as the beautiful San Juan mountains rising up behind the Cimarron River Valley.

Morrow Point Reservoir, Cimarron Valley and the San Juans

At the bottom is a picnic and/or tent camping area, complete with tables, grills and restrooms. Also at the bottom is a boat dock. The Boy Scouts sometimes choose Hermit's Rest for a beginning backpacking trip. The difficulty in this hike occurs when you must return uphill, perhaps during the heat of the day, and after having already hiked the three miles downhill. The good news is that the grade lessens the farther you climb uphill. I would suggest taking this hike during the cooler fall weather when there are the gorgeous colors of the red oak and yellow aspen.

CRYSTAL CREEK TRAIL
USGS Cimarron
TH Highway 92
SE 8500'
TVG 400'
RT 5 miles
EASY TO MODERATE

The Crystal Creek Trail is the furthest out on Highway 92, and the parking area is just a wide pullout next to the highway. This trail is great, a combination of uphill and downhill, making it pleasant both coming and going. Expect to walk through pines, junipers, aspen and scrub oak, interspersed with occasional sagebrush and many pretty wildflowers. Near the end of the trail, there is a split, with the right fork going to an overlook of the Crystal Reservoir, and the left fork going to the top of a rise for a better view of the West Elk Mountains. It is definitely easy to visit both of these areas. I think the most outstanding feature of this hike is the chance to see the contrast of the Gunnison Country by viewing the steep canyons and cliffs in the foreground and the spectacular, jagged peaks of the high San Juan Mountains in the background.

Beautiful view extending to the San Juans from the Crystal Creek Trail

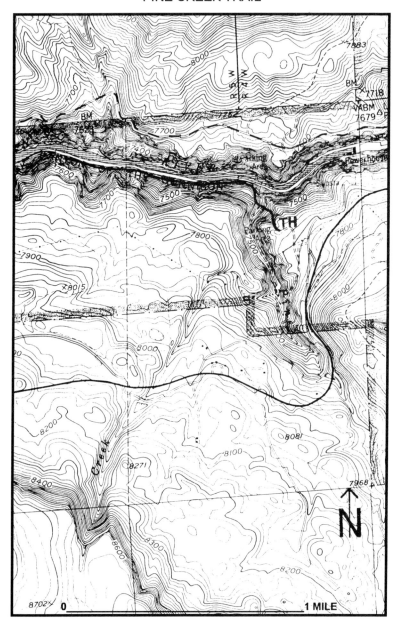

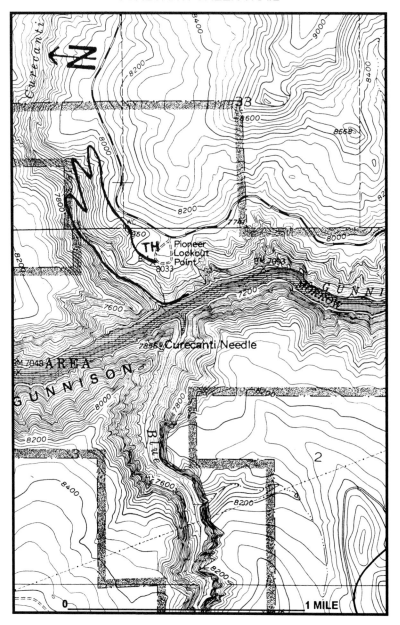

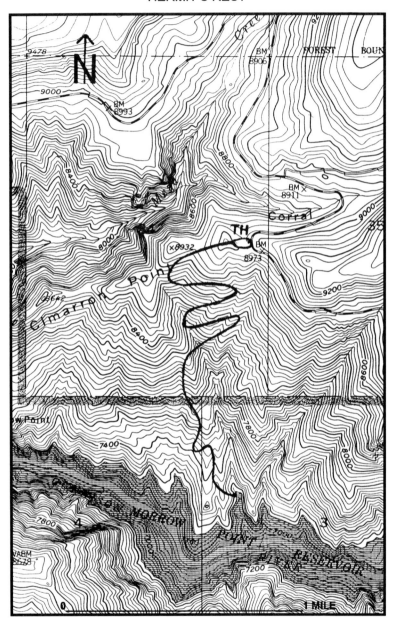

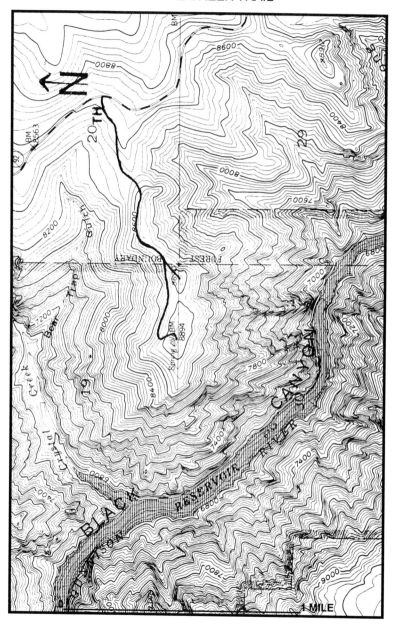

SOUTH BALDY MOUNTAIN 12,380'
MIDDLE BALDY MOUNTAIN 12,598'
MIDDLE BALDY 12,709'
NORTH BALDY MOUNTAIN 12,850'

USGS West Elk Peak

TH Rainbow Lake Road

SE 10,982'

TVG 1400' South Baldy

RT 6 miles

MODERATE

TVG 2120' Middle Baldy Mountain

TVG 2320' Middle Baldy

RT 10 miles

MODERATE TO STRENUOUS

TVG 2690' North Baldy Mountain

RT 12 miles

STRENUOUS

Continue driving past Rainbow Lake to the Rainbow Lake Trailhead located at the road end. The trail wanders through an old, dark, and sometimes wet forest for about a mile to a larger stream crossing. This crossing is no problem, and afterwards the trail borders a marshy area for a little less than a mile, climbing gradually upwards until it begins to flatten near a small stagnant lake. This whole large area is blanketed with Marsh Marigolds. A trail which goes around the east side of the Baldies takes off to the right at this lake. If you miss the trail, South Baldy is quite visible anyway.

It is only useful to be on the trail for a short distance to climb South Baldy. Follow the trail uphill just to the point where it starts down again, then follow the ridge you are on to the summit. From the summit of South Baldy, you will be able to see both of the Middle Baldies and can plan a route to them. When we were on top of South Baldy, there was a large herd of elk below us in the connecting saddle of South Baldy and Middle Baldy Mountain. On the Middle Baldies, the tundra is covered with Sky Pilots and Old Man of the Mountain Sunflowers, creating an impressive blue and yellow against the green of the alpine tundra. There are also quite a few Forget-Me-Nots on the Baldies. I was delighted to find a pretty little purple Pygmy Bitterroot near the summit of Middle Baldy. From the summit, there is a further continuation of a long, gentle ridge walk over to North Baldy. From both Middle and North Baldies is a gorgeous view of West Elk Peak. While approaching Middle Baldy, the rugged Elk Mountains beyond Crested Butte begin passing in review, with a really fine view of 14,265', Castle Peak.

Mary Pavillard on Middle Baldy Mountain with West Elk Peak

Regardless of how many Baldies included on your hike, I would recommend returning the same way you came, rather than following the trail which contours below on the east. We took the trail, and it follows around so many ridges, with ups and downs, that I think I would rather have regained the little bit of altitude to South Baldy and stayed up high. We were lucky to see another elk herd in the marshy area on the way back. Black Bear and Mountain Lions are often seen in the West Elk Wilderness.

Rainbow Lake, which is passed on the way to the trailhead, is also a scenic place to spend some time. The fishing can be quite good since the lake supports Rainbow, Browns, Brook and Cutthroat Trout.

CURECANTI & THE WEST ELKS

Elk Dance

"Look", she whispered with a gasp
Just as my eyes fixed on the ground,
Wondering who might have left this scat
My eyes rise
a herd of Elk
My heart jumps as I behold this blessing
I am wholly transfixed
More and more beasts appear
Have they seen us yet, I wonder?
What great fortune allows me this seat in this theater of Nature and God?
The dance proceeds
A power struggle between the leaders ensues
They pull right and then back round to the left
No time to argue
A decision is made
Up through the willows
Over the rocks
The trail looks impassable to the human eye
There is clearly no hesitation
So many bodies
So much mass
Yet their movement is weightless
With a magnificent finale they disappear down the ridge line
Brilliant silhouettes leaping and glissading down the summer snow
We hike along their trail
Letting the elk medicine sink in
Hours later we meet the herd again
There is a moment before our scent reaches them
One head comes up
Ears erect
Simultaneously they all turn and fly away
Another glimpse, Elk magic revisited

— Mary Pavillard

100

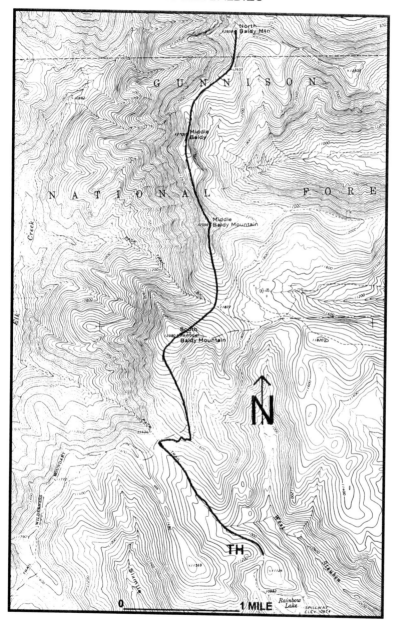

COAL MESA TRAIL
USGS Big Soap Park
TH Soap Park Road at Soap Creek Campground
SE 7740'
TVG 1220'
RT 4 miles
MODERATE

The trailhead is located at the north end of Soap Creek Campground. Turn left at the sign which indicates the horse corral, and keep driving until reaching the trailhead. This hike will encompass the first two miles of the Coal Mesa Trail which provides a nice excursion to see some of the gorgeous pinnacles of West Elk Breccia. Immediately after the trailhead, there is a foot bridge across Soap Creek. This creek supports Rainbow, Browns, Cutthroat and Brook Trout. After the bridge, the trail is relatively flat for a little over a mile and stays fairly close to Cow Creek. Hikers interested in fishing Cow Creek can expect to find Rainbow, Browns and Cutthroat. Along the trail there are many Ponderosa Pine and Engleman Spruce trees, with occasional Douglas Fir and aspen. The lower foliage consists of sagebrush, Gambel Oak, and Wild Rose.

West Elk Breccia near Soap Creek Campground

When the trail begins to climb upwards, you will leave Cow Creek by turning to the right and going up several switchbacks to reach the top of the ridge. From this higher aspect, the views of the pinnacles are particularly lovely. Just below the top of this ridge, the trail will join with the trail which comes up from the Ponderosa Campground along Coal Creek. The Coal Mesa Trail is another hike which can be very beautiful during the fall colors.

To extend the length of this hike, it is possible to make a loop up to Rock Spring at about 10,200' by following the Coal Creek drainage up and coming back along the ridge past Poison Spring. The Poison Spring Trail will return to the ridge of the Coal Mesa Trail. This loop would add about 5.5 miles to the Coal Mesa Hike.

Bighorn Sheep can often be seen in the cliffs across from Soap Creek Campground. During the summer of 1995, the Campground Host reported seeing Mountain Lions trailing behind the sheep. Many people have mentioned seeing cats, or their tracks, in the West Elks.

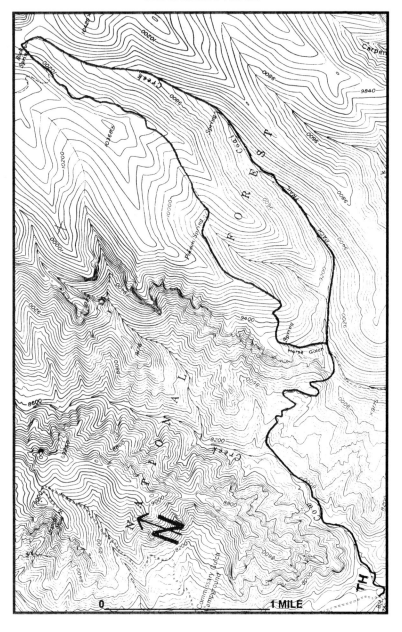

LAKE CITY AREA

The silver of the San Juan Mountains lured many prospectors into the area of the Lake Fork of the Gunnison River. Although Lake City was a mining "boom town" between 1876 and 1881, it was isolated from other towns and supply centers. Mining supplies had to be brought over, and through, the mountains by rough wagon roads such as Engineer and Cinnamon Passes, the Saguache and San Juan Toll Road, and the Antelope Park and Lake City Wagon Toll Road (Slumgullion Pass). It was August of 1889, before the rails of the Denver & Rio Grande Railroad were continued from Gunnison and reached Lake City. To drive to Lake City from Gunnison, go west on Highway 50 to the intersection with Highway 149 leading to Lake City.

From the last stoplight west of Gunnison, trailheads and roads are the following distances along Highway 149:

Intersection Highway 50 and Highway 149 is 8.7 miles
Powderhorn (CR 27) is 25.9 miles
Indian Creek (CR 58) is 29.6 miles
  Powderhorn Lakes TH is 10 miles
Blue Creek/Alpine Plateau Road is 43 miles
  Little Elk Creek TH is 3 miles
  Alpine Guard Station is 10 miles
  Big Blue Campground is 10.5 miles
  Big Blue TH is 11.4 miles
Independence Gulch TH is 48.7 miles
Lake City is 53.8 miles

HENSON CREEK

Henson Creek Road (CR 20), once the Henson Creek and Uncompahgre Toll Road, is also part of the Alpine Loop Scenic Byway heading west out of Lake City. The road, located 2 blocks north of Highway 149, was built right next to Henson Creek in a narrow valley, and does provide a very scenic drive. The road passes the Ute-Ule Mine, one of the major mines of Lake City. The veins of this mine were discovered by Henry Henson and 3 other prospectors in August of 1871. At the old site of Capitol City, 9.1 miles up Henson Creek, the road branches, with the left branch leading toward Engineer Pass and the right one going up North Henson Creek.

Trailheads and roads turning off the Henson Creek road are the following distances from the west edge of Lake City:

Alpine Gulch TH is 2.6 miles
North Henson Creek Road (FR 870) is 9.1 miles
Matterhorn Creek Road is 11.1 miles

LAKE SAN CRISTOBAL
LAKE FORK VALLEY

Lake San Cristobal, formed by the Slumgullion earthflow, is at the beginning of the valley leading up to Cinnamon Pass, an old road (4-wheel) over to Animas Forks. There were several mining settlements high up in this Lake Fork Valley. The old townsite of Sherman is below the shelf road into the portion of the higher valley known as Burrows Park. This area of the valley is named after early prospector, Charles Burrows. Small mining camps like Whitecross, Burrows Park (same name as the valley), Tellurium, and Argentum were all located in this area. Two buildings remain at the Silver Creek and Grizzly Gulch Trailheads which lead to some 14,000' peaks. The old town of Carson, partially restored, lies up a side valley known as Wager Gulch.

From the south edge of Lake City, trailheads and roads are the following distances:

Lake San Cristobal Road is 1.7 miles
Williams Creek TH is 8.5 miles
Cinnamon Pass Turnoff is 13.9 miles
Grizzly Gulch TH is 18.0 miles
Cooper Creek TH is 18.8 miles
Sherman Townsite is 14.6 miles
Cataract Gulch TH is 15.1 miles

SLUMGULLION

Highway 149 continues on from Lake City over Slumgullion and Spring Creek Passes toward Creede. In 1240 A.D., over 700 years ago, a massive earthflow of water-saturated clay and dirt gave way from the western edge of Cannibal Plateau and moved down the mountain, past the area which today is the Slumgullion Pass Road, and on down into the valley. This huge earthflow made a natural dam on the Lake Fork River and created Lake San Cristobal. Slumgullion Pass most likely is named for the stew called Slumgullion which was commonly made by the miners. However, the word slumgullion actually does refer to a foul-smelling, yellow mixture, and that definition also fits the smelly, yellow-colored clays of the Slumgullion earthflow. Be sure to drive into the Windy Point Overlook on Slumgullion Pass to see the beautiful panorama surrounding Lake City.

From the south side of Lake City, trailheads and roads on the Slumgullion Pass Road (Highway 149) are the following distances:

Windy Point is 8 miles
Cebolla Creek Road (FR 788) is 9.2 miles
    Deer Lakes Cmpgrnd (Devil's Lake) is 2.7 miles
    Brush Creek TH is 5.3 miles
    Rough Creek TH is 10.2 miles
    Mineral Creek Road is 11.4 miles
      Mineral Creek TH is 11.9 miles
    Powderhorn Park TH is 11.9 miles
    Cathedral (Los Pinos Road) is 15.2 miles
    Powderhorn is 31.1 miles
Summit Slumgullion Pass is 10.1miles
Oleo Ranch Turnoff is 15.4 miles
    Tumble Creek & Cebolla TH are 2 miles
Spring Creek Pass (Baldy Cinco TH) is 16.9 miles

The Slumgullion Earthflow

BIG BLUE CREEK TO FALL CREEK
SILVER MOUNTAIN 13,714'

USGS Sheep Mountain, Uncompahgre Peak
TH Big Blue Campground
SE 9700'
DAY 1 MODERATE
TVG 1700 (8.5 miles)
DAY 2 MODERATE TO STRENUOUS
TVG 1360' (7.3 miles)
TVG 2360' Silver Mountain (8.3 miles)
DAY 3 MODERATE
TVG 300' (7.7 miles)
RT 23.5 miles

The trailhead for this gentle, remote backpack is a mile south of Big Blue Campground on the Alpine Plateau Road. Begin by hiking up the Big Blue Trail, which passes first through beautiful Engelman Spruce and open parks and then up to high alpine tundra. Fishing for Brookies and Cutthroat is reportedly good in Big Blue Creek and Slide Lake, and numerous choices await for setting up camp. After about 8.5 miles, the Big Blue Trail will intersect with the trail coming from Nellie Creek. Be sure to go right at this intersection to reach the Fall Creek drainage. After the intersection, the trail climbs to a pass at 12,760' between 13,714', Silver Mountain and an unnamed 13,051' peak which lies at the head of the Fall Creek drainage. If you are interested in climbing either of these 2 peaks, this is the time to drop packs and do it. I would recommend camping high in the Blue Creek drainage the day before this portion of the trip, in order to get an early start for the peaks.

As the trail passes the side of Silver Mountain and drops down to about 12,400', you will come to the intersection of the Little Cimarron and Fall Creek Trails. Head down into the valley to your right on the Fall Creek Trail if you wish to end up at your car! Once down into the valley, the Fall Creek Trail continues through a long, relatively flat, open park. The trail is never far never far from Fall Creek which supports Colorado River Native Cutthroat. Unless fishing, it is important to stay on the trail, as the area in the center of the park is wetlands. The trail is marked with trail posts guiding you across two stream crossings. I recommend carrying crossing shoes on this trip. At the north end of the park, you will leave Fall Creek and climb up a small rise on the left into the Firebox Creek drainage.

13,051' Unnamed Peak at the head of Fall Creek drainage

Just before the trail goes over to Firebox Creek, you may notice the top of a jagged canyon where Fall Creek continues. Here the creek falls 800' to the valley floor. The top of the falls is a very dangerous area. I DO NOT recommend that you attempt to view the falls from the top for two reasons: 1. You can't see the falls. 2. The edge of the cliffs at the top of the falls slant downward on loose gravel over rocks. If it is important to you to be able to see the falls, bushwhack up the lower Fall Creek drainage from the Big Blue Trail to the base of the falls.

Firebox Creek is small and gentle, flowing through a long, flat park flanked with tall, stately spruce trees. The trail goes through the park on the east side. After traversing up and down a small hump and entering still another smaller park, there is a gorgeous place to camp, right at the first of the park near some smaller trees. At the end of this park, the trail comes out to a parking lot at the Fall Creek Trailhead, which can be reached on the Little Cimarron Road.

At the Fall Creek Trailhead, continue past it on the trail to Failes Creek. There is a little confusion, as the sign for the Failes Creek Trail points to the parking lot. There is a small branch of the trail leaving the parking lot and joining the continuation of the trail which you have been following. At any rate, the trail heads down the Failes Creek drainage to another park. At the next trail intersection in the park, go right up over the small ridge, and then down steeply for about 900 vertical feet to the Alpine Guard Station. The station is about a half mile from the Big Blue Campground. Hike to the campground and then the additional .9 mile to your car at the Big Blue Trailhead. Brookies swim in both Firebox Creek and Failes Creek. Be sure to take a map and compass on this trip.

Gorgeous campsite near little Firebox Creek

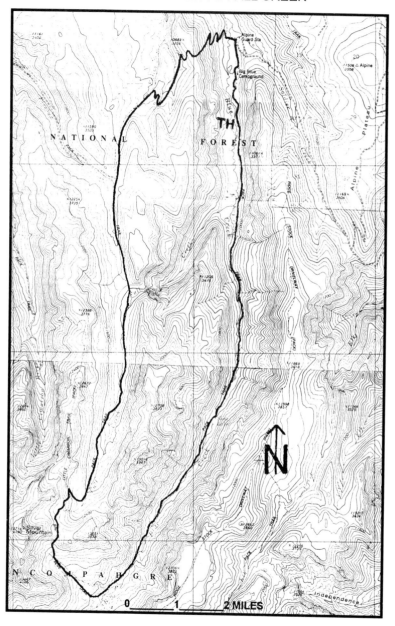

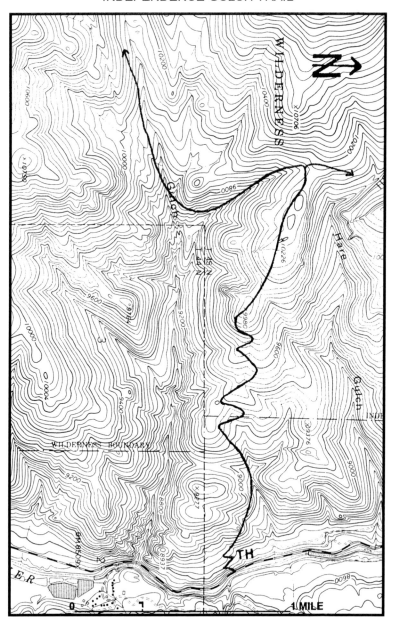

INDEPENDENCE GULCH TRAIL

USGS Lake City
TH Highway 149 north of Lake City
SE 8500'
TVG 1700'
RT 4.5 miles
MODERATE

Hiking the Independence Gulch Trail for 2.25 miles to the intersection with Little Elk Trail makes for a pleasant and beautiful afternoon hike. From the parking area on Highway 149, the trail climbs very steeply up the first short hillside, after which the grade becomes a bit gentler. Much of this trail is comprised of switchbacks as it passes through sage, juniper, Ponderosa Pine, aspen, and Douglas Fir, as well as many open, grassy meadows. The view across the Lake Fork Valley to Cannibal Plateau is grand. Until the intersection of trails, the trail remains a bit north of Independence Gulch itself, but occasionally has a beautiful overlook into this area. The meadows are filled with pretty flowers, especially a lot of Lupine.

View towards Cannibal Plateau from Independence Gulch Trail

From the trail intersection, it is possible to hike further on Little Elk Trail, or for a longer hike, continue for another 2 miles on the Independence Gulch Trail until it joins the Larson Lakes Trail just north of the lakes. The distance to reach Larson Lakes from this trail is about a mile longer than the 4 mile distance of the Larson Lakes Trail above the cemetery. The Little Elk Trail can also be reached from the Alpine Plateau Road.

Thea Nordling and Laura McClow enjoy a rest on Independence Gulch Trail

CRYSTAL LAKE 11,760'
CRYSTAL PEAK 12,933'

USGS Lake City
TH IOOF Cemetery Lake City
SE 8800'
TVG 3000' to lake
TVG 4100' with peak
RT 8 miles to lake
STRENUOUS
RT 10 miles with peak
VERY STRENUOUS

The trailhead for Crystal Lake is just north of Lake City. There is a sign on Highway 149 indicating the Hinsdale IOOF Cemetery. Turn west at this sign onto Balsam Drive and continue following it until just past the cemetery where you will reach a sign for the Crystal and Larson Lakes Trailhead. Park here and begin walking further up Balsam Drive, through private property on either side of the road, until you arrive at a US Forest Service Gate. At this gate, the left fork beyond the gate goes to Crystal Lake and the right fork is signed for Thompson Lake, which continues on to Larson Lakes.

The trail to Crystal Lake follows portions of a steep, old jeep road which went all the way to the lake. The road is now closed to motor vehicles and the trail is more gently rerouted around several sections of the old road. Much of this picturesque hike is in dense aspen groves joined by open grassy areas. Near the bottom, the trail winds through some lovely Ponderosa Pines, and as the trail nears the lake, there are spruce and fir trees. Throughout the forests are many, many Heartleaf Arnica. About 2/3 of the way to Crystal Lake, the trail passes by a pretty little lake called Hay Lake. Hey, a lake! After Hay Lake, the first brief glimpse of the summit of Crystal Peak is seen, and as the trail begins the last uphill to the lake, more and more of the peak begins to come into view.

Just before reaching Crystal Lake, there is a post cairn on the right side of the trail. Look across the open meadow and you will see a line of these cairns marking the trail which, after another 3.5 miles, will intersect the Larson Lakes Trail above Larson Lakes. A nice backpacking trip can be enjoyed by returning to the car via the Larson Lakes Trail. Expect to find Brookies in Crystal Lake.

Crystal Peak above Crystal Lake

An old cabin still remains at Crystal Lake, although its roof is no longer functional. From the cabin, look across the lake to 12,933', Crystal Peak and see the route to the summit. The peak consists of a lower wide shelf which connects with the summit ridge. To begin the climb, skirt around the northern arm of the lake, then climb through the trees to the top of the shelf. Cross this wide, grassy shelf and climb steeply up the grass and through easy rocks to the ridge directly in front of you. Follow the ridge to the summit. Sorry, but the view is really not available until on the summit. However, the panoramic view from the summit is outstanding, with Uncompahgre Peak being especially gorgeous. Enjoy this view, it is one of the best!

CRYSTAL LAKE & CRYSTAL PEAK

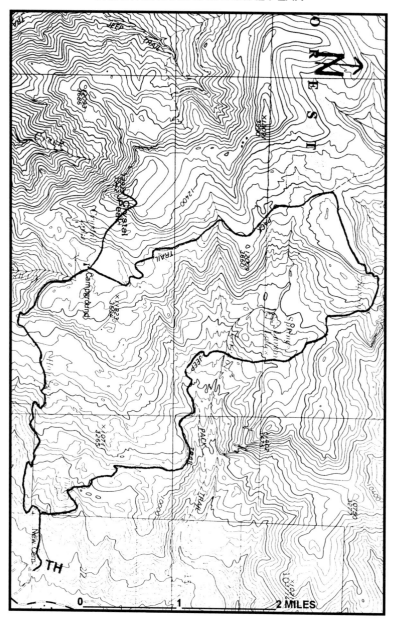

MATTERHORN CREEK
MATTERHORN PEAK 13,590'

USGS Uncompahgre, Wetterhorn
TH North Henson Creek Road
SE 10,400'
TVG 2000' end of the valley
RT 6 miles
MODERATE TO DIFFICULT
TVG 3190' with Matterhorn Peak
RT 8 miles
STRENUOUS

While still on the North Henson Creek Road, there is a nice pullout for cars where the short, 4-wheel drive road heads up Matterhorn Creek to the official trailhead at the wilderness boundary. Matterhorn Creek is one of my favorite places. A little before the trailhead you will get a brief glimpse of Matterhorn Peak. Beyond the trailhead, you will be following the Ridge Stock Driveway through a pretty forest to the first stream crossing, a tributary of Matterhorn Creek. After another short distance next to Matterhorn Creek, the trail has a couple of switchbacks leading to high up on the hillside above the creek. While hiking this section, the top of Wetterhorn Peak just peeks over another mountain on the left.

M. A. & Amanda Tarr high in Matterhorn Basin with Uncompahgre Peak

At about 11,600', the trail leaves the trees and enters a very beautiful basin. There are some lovely campsites which are not far from the creek over to the left in the basin. Matterhorn Peak is visible as soon as the trail enters the basin, and as you go higher, more and more of 14,015' Wetterhorn Peak will come into view. Finally, both Matterhorn and Wetterhorn and their connecting ridge can be seen guarding this basin on its west side. Continuing up the trail to the north will provide a grand view of Uncompahgre Peak across a high yoke joining El Paso Creek to the south and the East Fork of the Cinnamon River to the north. From here it is fun to climb Matterhorn Peak up the steep grassy slopes. The last 200' are a rock scramble to the summit and one beautiful view!

The summit cone of Matterhorn Peak

Matterhorn Peak also sports some fine glissading or skiing in May or June. When on snow, remember to start early, do your climbing or skiing and be out of the basin by noon. I have experienced some terrific, waistdeep postholing in this basin when it is full of snow!!

In early June, four of us drove to Matterhorn Creek for a ski trip to Matterhorn Peak. We parked my jeep at about 6:30 am and returned at about 2:30 pm. The next day, my son and I discovered a visitor had taken up residence in my jeep engine. A lady marmot had moved in and safely traveled 70 miles home with us. She had made her presence known by exploring our garage the first night; however, after her initial tour of the garage, she steadfastly refused to leave the jeep. Finally, after two and a half days, and with the assistance of the local vet, Dr. Jim Noone, she was extricated, unharmed, from the jeep and returned to the wilderness.

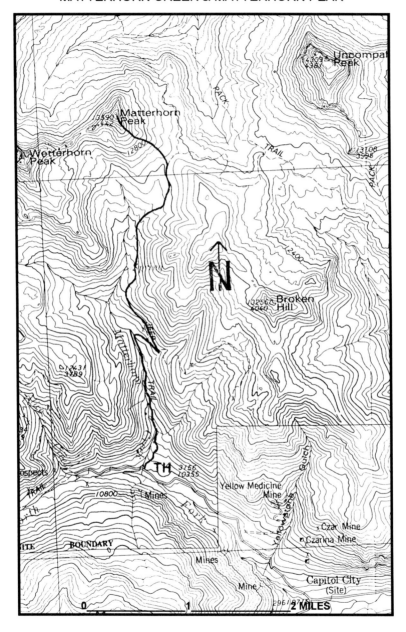

ALPINE GULCH TRAIL
GRASSY MOUNTAIN 12,821'
RED MOUNTAIN 12,826'

USGS Lake City, Lake San Cristobal
TH Henson Creek Road
SE 9000'
TVG 2800' to first saddle
RT 11 miles first saddle
STRENUOUS
TVG 3800' to Red Mountain
RT 13+ miles
VERY STRENUOUS
TVG 3400' to Grassy Mountain saddle
RT 12 miles
VERY STRENUOUS
TVG 3800' to Grassy Mountain
RT 13 miles
VERY STRENUOUS

Parking for the Alpine Gulch Trail is on the big, wide area at the side of Henson Creek Road just below the BLM Trail sign. The trail initially drops off abruptly from the edge of the road, and winds down to a foot bridge across Henson Creek. This bridge is not visible from the road.

The most notable features of the Alpine Gulch Trail are the seven stream crossings, occurring in groups of two, in the first 2.5 miles of the hike. I can not recommend this trail when the water is high during the run-off season. At this time, some of the log crossings might be missing or too dangerous. The logs are at least one meter above the water and can feel a little shakey. I recommend holding a long pole down in the water to help maintain balance when using these high crossings. Aside from negotiating these crossings, the trail is very beautiful, winding up the narrow Alpine Gulch canyon between high cliffs.

The first 1.5 miles of the trail are on private land and it is important to remain on the trail. Alpine Gulch is not recommended for fishing.

Right at the 8th stream crossing the trail branches, with left going up the East Fork and right going across the water and up the West Fork. Take the East Fork Trail. Although there are several more stream crossings, they are quite small and easy to accomplish. The trail continues for about 2.5 miles by following the East Fork of Alpine Gulch between the lower flanks of both Grassy Mountain and Red Mountain. The next one half mile portion of the trail goes through trees up several switchbacks to reach a definite saddle between the two mountains. There is evidence of a major camp at this saddle, although water is not readily available. To reach a higher saddle on Grassy Mountain, continue on the trail to the right as it climbs the ridge up to treeline and then is marked by cairns in the high alpine tundra. It is quite easy to see this saddle on Grassy Mountain by climbing just a short distance up on the Red Mountain side above the first saddle. Beautiful views exist from the Grassy Mountain Saddle which can also be reached by hiking the Williams Creek Trail from the other side. 12,821', Grassy Mountain can also be climbed from this high saddle.

Looking from Red Mountain towards Grassy Mountain on the far left

From the first saddle between Red and Grassy Mountains, it is not possible to see Red Mountain summit, but rather the 12,601', subsidiary peak. The true summit of Red Mountain is first seen from the ridge above the saddle. To climb Red Mountain, first climb the subsidiary peak or contour around it and then climb to the summit of Red. Although the rock feels a bit unstable on the climb to Red Mountain, it actually doesn't move all that much. The view from 12,826', Red Mountain includes Uncompahgre, Matterhorn, Coxcomb and Wetterhorn Peaks. The junky pipes on the Red Mountain summits are the leftovers of some core drilling which was done in the 1970's to ascertain what was below and inside Red Mountain.

Wetterhorn, Coxcomb, Matterhorn and Uncompahgre Peaks from Red Mtn

ALPINE GULCH, GRASSY MTN. & RED MTN.

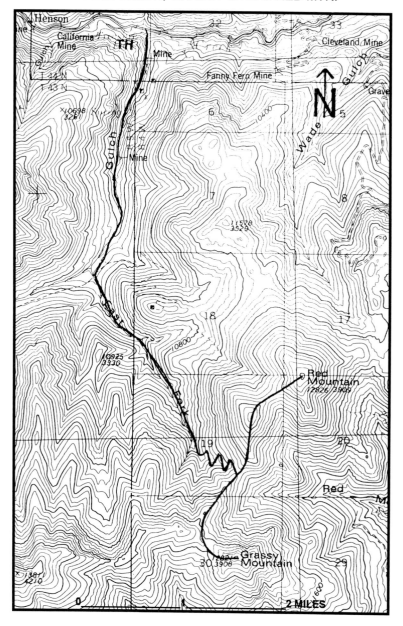

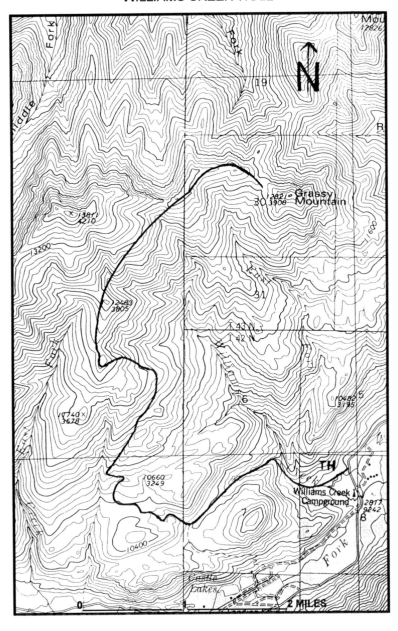

WILLIAMS CREEK TRAIL
USGS Lake San Cristobal
TH Lake San Cristobal Road
SE 9185'
TVG 3000' to ridge
RT 9 miles
STRENUOUS
TVG 3300' to Grassy Mountain Saddle
RT 15 miles
VERY STRENUOUS

From the trailhead on the Lake San Cristobal Road, it would be a very long day hike to go the 7.5 miles to Grassy Mountain Saddle, although the view is exceptional. An easier hike of about 4.5 miles goes just to the ridge above treeline, and offers a beautiful view across the valley to the Continental Divide, Wager Gulch and the old town of Carson. Although the terrain varies from talus to meadow to forest, the trail is always in or near aspen, making this hike a nice choice for a fall color hike. Along with the aspen, first you will walk through a Ponderosa Pine forest, followed by an old growth forest of Douglas Fir, with the most incredibly huge old trees. When in these old trees, it feels like you are surrounded by grandparents. There are two minor stream crossings, after which the trail parallels and crosses a bog area until it joins an old jeep road. At places where there might be a question as to the route, the BLM has placed signs pointing to the trail.

Once on the old jeep road, after a short steep uphill, the trail opens into a flat meadow. In this meadow there is a grand view of 14,001', Sunshine Peak, and by walking off the trail into the meadow it is possible to see 14,034', Redcloud Peak. After this meadow, get ready for a steady grunt uphill to treeline. Just before treeline, when the road turns to the west, you will be able to finally see Grassy Mountain and the saddle, some three walking miles distant. At the end of the jeep road, look for rock cairns marking the route, if your destination is Grassy Mountain or its saddle via the tundra ridge walk. There is a nice spot for camping where the trail joins the old jeep road for those wishing to go to Grassy Mountain with an overnight to break up the trip.

CATARACT GULCH WATERFALL 11,200'
CATARACT LAKE 12,082'
CONTINENTAL DIVIDE 12,400'

USGS Redcloud Peak, Polecreek Mountain
TH Beyond Sherman townsite at Cataract Gulch
SE 9630'
TVG 1570' Waterfall
RT 4.4 miles
MODERATE
TVG 2450' Cataract Lake
RT 7.2 miles
MODERATE TO STRENUOUS
TVG 2770' Continental Divide
RT 8.2 miles
STRENUOUS

The Cataract Gulch Trail departs the parking area beyond the Sherman Townsite by crossing Cottonwood Creek via a high log bridge. When Steven Wells and I did it, one of two logs was missing, making for a scary crossing on one bouncy log. I chose to wade the creek. The trail climbs rapidly up into the gulch through dense spruce and fir forest, carpeted with the cheerful Heartleaf Arnica and an occasional Columbine. There are some long, gentle switchbacks which replace an old steeper trail during the first really steep portions. The trail climbs steadily until the head of the gulch, but when it parallels Cataract Creek in the upper half of the gulch, both sides are flanked by abundant Colorado Columbine, Bluebells, Larkspur, Indian Paintbrush and Twinberry. An old log cabin, ore car and rusty, old rails give evidence of the mining in this area. The upper portion of the trail in the gulch also has two noteworthy waterfalls, the higher one being quite spectacular. For a shorter hike with gorgeous scenery, I could recommend hiking Cataract Gulch just up to the second waterfall. Immediately above the waterfall is a nice wooded area which is often used for camping.

Second Waterfall on Cataract Gulch Trail

At the head of the gulch the trail continues on through talus, alpine meadows and willows. The route hugs the east side of the valley, an important fact to remember when trying to locate it on the return, as the trail vanishes just before the lakes. As you look at the head of the valley from the trail, the largest lake is located right under the high point with the prominent rock nose. There are a few Brookies in the lake.

LAKE CITY AREA

If you wish to climb higher, it is best to stay to the north and west on the hillside above the large lake in order to avoid marshy areas. The Continental Divide is south of the lake above the rock nose, and it is well worth the effort to climb up above the lake and enjoy the view. The hillside NW of the lake was just covered with Rosy Paintbrush in one area! The entire area above treeline had lots of Marsh Marigolds and a large number of Explorer's Gentian. Above the lake I also saw some Moss Gentian and some particularly beautiful Stonecrop.

View of Sunshine Peak from Continental Divide above Cataract Lake

CATARACT GULCH TRAIL

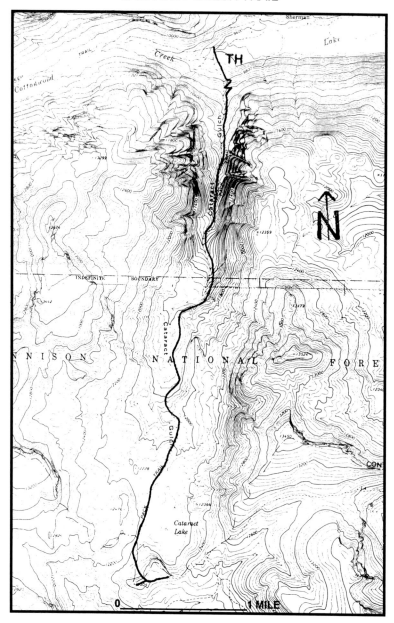

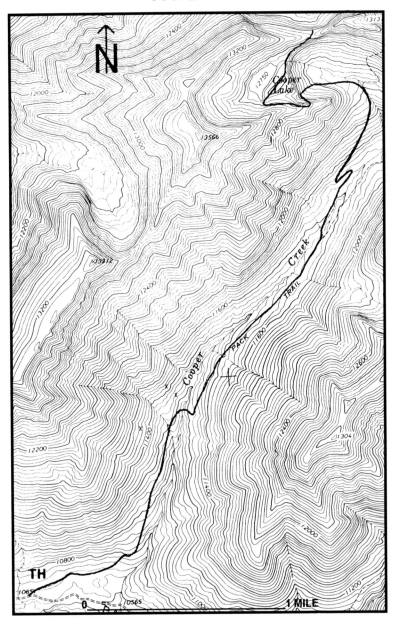

COOPER LAKE 12,750'
USGS Redcloud Peak
TH Cinnamon Pass Road above Silver Creek TH
SE 10,560'
TVG 2200'
RT 7.2 miles
MODERATE TO STRENUOUS

The trailhead for this hike is .8 mile beyond the Silver Creek and Grizzly Gulch Trailheads; however, there is no sign marking the trail, just an old closed road and a parking area. Hike on this old road, and after the first little uphill, you will come to a register box. The trail is mostly a two track road to the first stream crossing, as the road leads to an old mining operation. Once on the east side of Cooper Creek, you will pass by the cabins of the mine. Please respect private property when passing by, as that helps with continued access for trails which pass through private property. After about 2.2 miles and 1000 vertical feet, the trail crosses back to the west side of the creek. As the trail follows Cooper Creek up the valley, there are beautiful views of the unnamed peaks on either side. It would be easy to climb up to many of the summits or to take a high ridge walk. We saw a small herd of elk high on the west side.

Whitecross Mountain and Handies Peak from high in Cooper Creek drainage

John Tarr near Cooper Lake with the route to Lee Smelter Gulch at far top left

Once the trail leaves the trees before the second stream crossing, it is possible to see the trail beyond as it climbs up into a basin. Do not expect to find the lake in the first basin, however, as it is up in a second basin. The trail to the first basin is flanked by beautiful Colorado Columbine, as well as many other pretty flowers. At the first basin, keep to the left and look for cairns marking the trail which goes south of the boggy area, and then climbs steeply up into the second basin. The lake remains hidden from sight until high up into the second basin. The Old Man of the Mountains Sunflower grows in the tundra by the lake. Even though the vertical gain after the second stream crossing is 1200' in 1.4 miles, this hike is truly worth the effort, as the lake is in a stunning setting at 12,750'. Those hikers who enjoy fishing can expect to find Colorado River Native Cutthroat and Brook Trout in the lake.

An additional short hike can be taken north of the outlet to the top of the ridge for a view down Lee Smelter Gulch below

Capitol City. Lee Smelter Gulch is named for George T. Lee, an 1880's resident of Capitol City who built a big, two-story, brick house and owned a smelting works on Henson Creek at the base of Lee Smelter Gulch.

Cooper Lake

SLOAN LAKE 12,900'
USGS Handies Peak
TH American Basin of Cinnamon Pass Road
SE 11,320'
TVG 1580'
RT 4.5 miles
MODERATE

      The entrance to beautiful American Basin is on the left of the first switchback of the Cinnamon Pass Road. Most passenger cars should be able to make it this far and there are a few places to park here. A 4-wheel drive road continues on for a short distance below the west slopes of 14,048', Handies Peak. Walk on this road, as it will soon turn into a trail, as it approaches American Basin with its spectacular, steep peaks.

135

Sloan Lake is at 12,900' on the high floor of this basin, directly below these peaks. Once you are heading east into the basin, stay south (right) on the trail with switchbacks up to this beautiful lake. Sloan Lake supports Cutthroat Trout for hikers wishing to fish. I would not recommend camping at Sloan Lake when there is ANY chance of thunderstorms as there is no protection. There are scenic places to camp just before the road turns into a trail. Sheep are grazed in the lower portions of American Basin late in the summer.

Ray, Grant and Alex Ruehle at Sloan Lake -- Photo by Nancy Ruehle

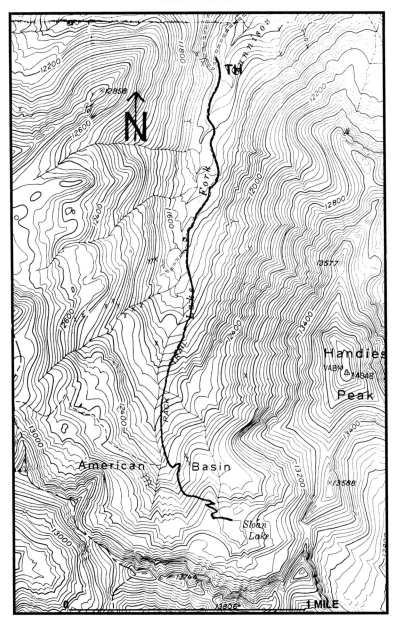

MINERAL CREEK TRAIL

USGS Mineral Mountain, Baldy Cinco
TH Cebolla Creek Road
SE 9200'
TVG 1200'
RT 10 miles to Cebolla Trail
RT 12 miles to East Mineral Creek
MODERATE

To reach the actual trailhead for Mineral Creek, turn at the sign on the Cebolla Creek Road and go for another one half mile. This is a very gentle hike, wandering up along Mineral Creek to the intersection with the Cebolla Trail at some beautiful beaver ponds. The first portion of the trail does not match the USGS map which shows the trail on the east side of Mineral Creek. It actually begins on the west side and remains there for about 2 miles, until the only big stream crossing. I would recommend crossing shoes for this creek, for although the crossing is quite easy, it is over boot tops even at the end of the season. Up until this crossing, and for a short distance afterwards, the trail is in grass and flower meadows with trees nearby. You will see a few Ponderosa Pine, and many Bristlecone Pine, Blue Spruce, Douglas Fir and aspen trees. An unnamed peak, rising to just over 13,000', dominates the view ahead on the first portion of the hike. Near the stream crossing, 12,097', Mineral Mountain comes into view on the left.

Mineral Mountain from the Mineral Creek Trail

After about 3 miles and at 9600', both the trail and Mineral Creek angle south. This is the first time you will feel like you are going uphill, although the grade is still not very steep. Through this section the trail is primarily in forest until the intersection with the Cebolla Trail. There are occasional views of the high peaks at the head of Mineral Creek, and the view becomes quite spectacular at the beaver ponds. Once at the Cebolla Trail intersection, it is but another fairly flat mile to the intersection with the East Mineral Creek Trail. This extra mile allows you to see more of the marvelous activity of the "busy beaver". Just before East Mineral Creek there is also a neat old cabin. Mineral Creek has German Brown and Snake River Cutthroat Trout. We did see elk on the trail on this hike.

EAST MINERAL CREEK & SKYLINE TRAIL

USGS Mineral Mountain, Baldy Cinco

TH Cebolla Creek Road

SE 9200'

DAY 1 MODERATE

TVG 1200' (6 miles)

DAY 2 MODERATE TO STRENUOUS

TVG 2100' (7 miles)

DAY 3 EASY TO MODERATE

TVG 0 downhill to trailhead (6 miles)

RT 19 miles

This backpacking trip provides a nice opportunity to hike part of the Skyline Trail high up on the Continental Divide without having to carry all your camping paraphernalia the entire way. First follow the directions for the Mineral Creek Hike to East Mineral Creek, where there are beautiful spots to set up basecamp.

Due to the high elevation of 12,500' reached during this hike, be sure to take the usual precautions for afternoon thunderstorms by starting the hike early in the day. The elevation gain from basecamp will be about 2000 feet. Start by hiking about 2.5 miles up the East Mineral Trail where it joins the Skyline Trail. Go west (right) on the Skyline Trail over the hump at about 12,200' and back down the Middle Mineral Creek drainage. If you are tired, it is possible to follow the trail back down Middle Mineral Creek to basecamp. This loop, however, continues to the West Mineral Creek drainage, reaching an elevation of 12,500' before dropping down. A portion of the trail coming down to West Mineral Creek is visible from the beaver ponds near basecamp. At the trail junction down to West Mineral Creek, the Skyline Trail will continue high along the Continental Divide before dropping down into the Tumble Creek drainage. Be sure to take the West Mineral Creek Trail down to reach your basecamp. The Skyline Trail, high in the tundra, is often vague and is marked with post cairns. Sometimes these cairns can be difficult to locate. I definitely recommend taking a map and compass on this hike.

Beaver lodge near the intersection of Cebolla and Mineral Creek Trails

140

MINERAL CREEK TO ROUGH CREEK
USGS Mineral Mountain, Baldy Cinco
TH Cebolla Creek Road
SE 9200'
DAY 1 MODERATE
TVG 1200' (5 miles)
DAY 2 MODERATE
TVG 1300 ' (5 miles)
DAY 3 EASY
TVG 0 (4.5 miles downhill)
RT 14.5 miles

This circle from Mineral Creek to Rough Creek makes a nice backpacking trip. Begin by following the directions for the hike up Mineral Creek. The first intersection with the Cebolla Trail is for the trail which goes over to Spring Creek, which is in the opposite direction from Rough Creek. Continue on the Mineral Creek Trail just a tad further and there will be a sign indicating the Cebolla Trail to Rough Creek. To locate the trail from this sign, look around for a tall trail marker and walk over to it. At this marker you will be able to see the remnants of an old bridge across Mineral Creek. The bridge leads to the Cebolla Trail. Since the intersection with the Cebolla Trail is in such a beautiful spot, I would recommend setting up camp in this vicinity. It is 5 miles to this intersection.

Thea Nordling on the old bridge leading to Mineral Park

Peggy Lue Reece tells me that the bridge on the Cebolla Trail was put in long ago by the sheep ranchers who used to drive the sheep along the Cebolla Trail. There is also a bridge abutment remaining at Rough Creek. It was necessary to build these bridges to be able to drive the sheep during high water.

The traverse over to Rough Creek passes through Mineral Park at 11,700'. To find reliable water for your next camp, it is necessary to descend from Mineral Park into the Rough Creek drainage, where there are beautiful campsites right next to the creek. The campsites are a very short distance up the Rough Creek Trail, rather than down towards the trailhead. On the switchbacks of the trail down to Rough Creek, you will pass by a very large squirrel midden, with the refuse of eaten spruce cones extending out into the trail. Also high in the switchbacks, it is possible to leave the trail and walk around the mountain briefly for the great view of Baldy Cinco up the head of the Rough Creek drainage. It is 6 miles along the Cebolla Trail to Rough Creek from Mineral Creek.

On the final day, it is only 3 miles down to the Rough Creek Trailhead on Cebolla Creek, however, your car is at the Mineral Creek Trailhead, 1.7 miles away. Walk or hitchhike to the Mineral Creek Road and then go the one half mile to the car.

ROUGH CREEK TRAIL
USGS Mineral Mountain
TH Cebolla Creek Road
SE 9200'
TVG 1400'
RT 6.5 to 8 miles
MODERATE

The destination for this hike is an incredible logging and water engineering area, all of which has been created by industrious little beavers. Begin at the Rough Creek Trailhead on the Cebolla Creek Road, and hike the first few switchbacks up to the meadow. This trail actually is in the trees most of the time, although open meadows are not far away. The first part of the trail passes through Ponderosa Pine and spruce trees. Throughout the walk there are always aspen trees, and up until the stream crossing, there are a lot of Bristlecone Pines. This hike just has a nice feel to it.

After approximately 3 miles, the Cebolla Trail will cross the Rough Creek Trail on its traverse from the Cochetopa to Quiet Valley. This is also where the Rough Creek Trail finally joins Rough Creek. The first intersection in the trail is where the Cebolla Trail comes down from Mineral Creek via Mineral Park. It joins and becomes one trail with the Rough Creek Trail through the stream crossing and then leaves the Rough Creek drainage to go over the ridge to Martinez Creek. The sign where Cebolla Trail leaves again is at the top of the hill across the creek. Expect to find Snake River Cutthroat in Rough Creek.

After the intersection with the Cebolla Trail, continue hiking on the Rough Creek Trail. In a very short distance, you will be able to see the marvelous work of the beaver, and it will be quite visible for at least a mile. Take time to inspect the teeth marks and wood chips where they have taken out some very large aspen trees. Note also, how baby aspen trees are already coming back in their heavily logged areas. I loved looking at the precision with which the beaver engineered their dams. The trail is relatively flat to the Cebolla Trail intersection, and the beaver work is just after, so I would recommend this as a great walk for kids.

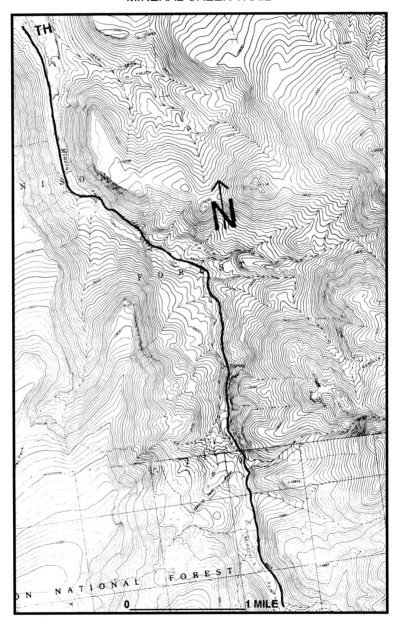

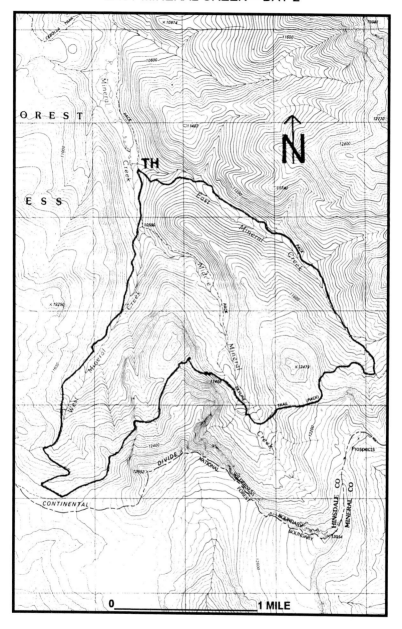

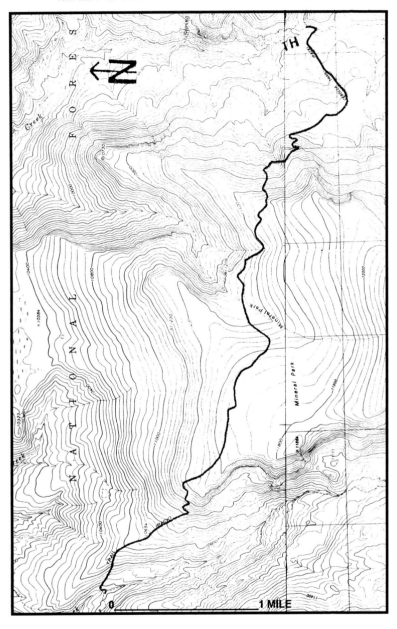

ROUGH CREEK TRAIL

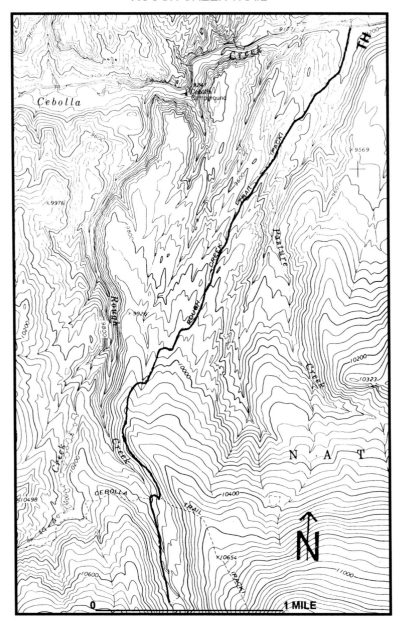

TUMBLE CREEK (Skyline) TRAIL
USGS Slumgullion Pass, Baldy Cinco
TH Quiet Valley off Slumgullion Pass
SE 10,300'
TVG 1900'
RT 10 miles
MODERATE TO STRENUOUS

Leave the Slumgullion Pass Road at the Oleo Ranch sign, and drive for 2 miles to reach the Tumble Creek Trailhead. It is a beautiful hike up Tumble Creek to the large cirque between Baldy Cinco and Baldy *no es* Cinco (See Baldy Cinco Hike). Baldy *no es* Cinco dominates the view for the first part of the hike and then slips out of view, leaving a view of the long ridge of lower summits which extend from it. Baldy Cinco, itself, will not be visible until the trail passes the end of this ridge. The only larger stream crossing is Cebolla Creek which is right at the trailhead. The place where we crossed had a board and it was during low water, but I would recommend bringing some crossing shoes. There are two more crossings of Tumble Creek higher up along the trail, and they are small. Brookies are the fish found in Tumble Creek.

The cirque between Baldy Cinco (left) and Baldy *no es* Cinco

148

Once you leave the trees and are in high, open meadows, the trail markers are difficult to locate and the trail is very vague. When in doubt, stay right at the edge of the willows until you are able to locate a marker or the trail. After the trail passes the end of the Baldy *no es* Cinco ridge, not only will you be able to see Baldy Cinco, but you should see a sign on a post. This sign says you are looking at Baldy Cinco. Try to pass behind the sign on the left to avoid a marshy area. There is a faint climbers trail going into the basin and it is possible to climb Baldy Cinco from this cirque. If your only goal is to climb the peak, I think it is easier to do so from Spring Creek Pass.

Continue following the trail up to approximately 12,200', where it passes the end of the ridge coming down from Baldy Cinco, and you will be able to look into the next beautiful cirque at the head of the Rough Creek drainage. This is really a breath-taking view and well worth the effort to see it. There is a good chance of seeing big game while on this hike.

TUMBLE CREEK TO ROUGH CREEK

USGS Baldy Cinco, Mineral Mountain, Slumgullion Pass
TH Quiet Valley off Slumgullion Pass
SE 10,300'
DAY 1 MODERATE TO DIFFICULT
TVG 1900' to Rough Creek 6 miles
DAY 2 EASY TO MODERATE
TVG 0 downhill to Cebolla Trail 5 miles
DAY 3 MODERATE
TVG 1000' on Cebolla Trail 6 miles
RT 17 miles

This is a beautiful backpacking trip with great alpine vistas. Follow the directions for the Tumble Creek Hike. Continue on the Tumble Creek Trail into the cirque beyond Baldy Cinco. Although the USGS map shows a trail through this cirque around to Rough Creek, we were not able to find one for approximately the last .75 of a mile. At the last, tall, easy to locate post, head left down through the tundra, but on the ridge above the willows until you can see a group of three signs marking the trail intersection of Rough Creek and Skyline Trails. Do not cross Rough Creek until you see these signs and you won't have to mess with the willows. The USGS map indicates a trail crossing prior to the intersection, but I couldn't find it, and it is easy to see the intersection from the open slopes across from it. Do not let assorted game trails confuse you regarding the Skyline Trail. It heads up through the valley at the far end of the cirque ridge, not in the middle of it. I recommend taking a map and compass with you on this trip. Near the trail intersection are beautiful camping spots.

Heading down to the intersection of Rough Creek and Skyline Trails

About half of the hike down Rough Creek to the Cebolla Trail is in open meadow with trail posts. The trail will stay a bit to the right of Rough Creek and you will need to watch for posts down near the water to find a crossing above some beaver ponds. If you miss the crossing, there is a faint trail until below the ponds, where you can, and must, cross before the stream enters the canyon. It is easy to pick up the trail markers on the left side of the creek. After a pleasant walk in a spruce forest, you will come to aspen and be able to see the work of the beavers as described in the Rough Creek Trail Hike. Continue past the beaver area to the intersection with the Cebolla Trail. Pick out a nice place to camp.

The last part of the hike is on the traversing Cebolla Trail which will return you to the Tumble Creek Trailhead. There is a small ridge to cross to reach Martinez Creek, after which there is another impressive beaver area. The trail then makes a steady climb up to a ridge at just over 11,000' before it descends to Round Park. This large park has plenty of trail markers to guide you around on the righthand edge. At the bottom of the park, the trail heads SW up a gentle incline and then down a series of steep switchbacks. When the trail comes out into the open you will be able to see the trailhead.

The incredible work of the beaver

TUMBLE CREEK TO ROUGH CREEK -- DAY 1

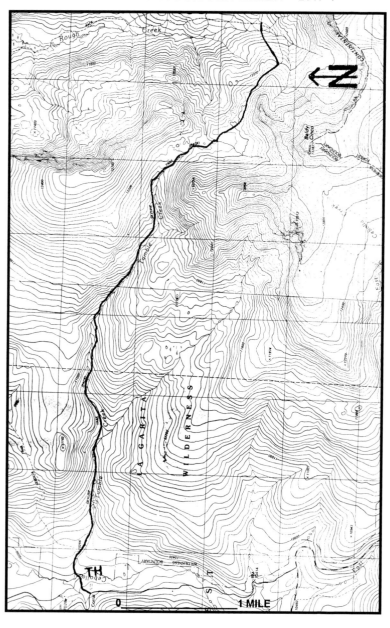

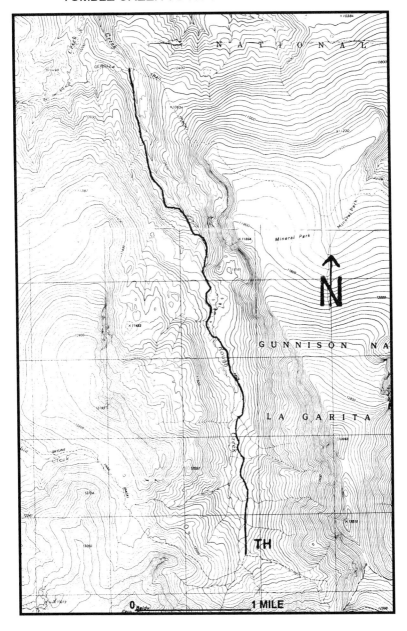

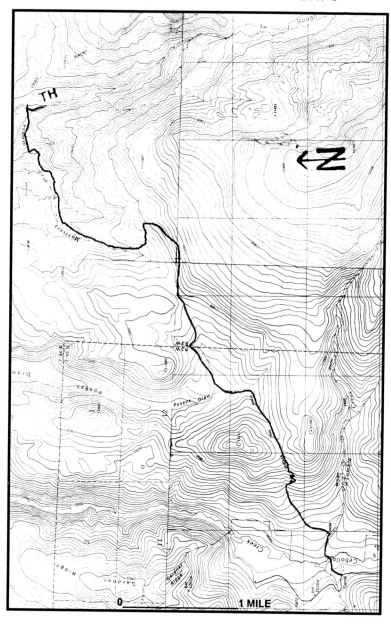

BALDY CINCO & BALDY no es CINCO

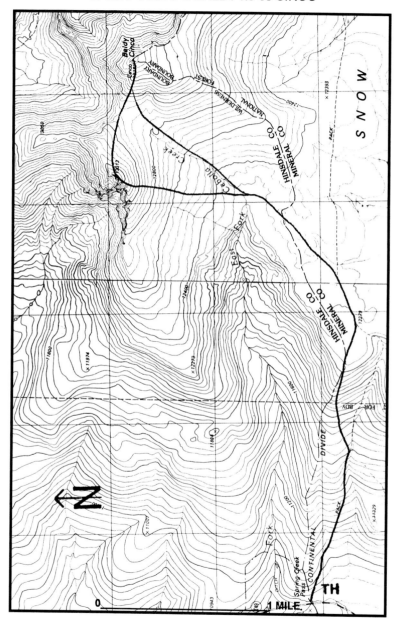

BALDY CINCO 13,383'
USGS Slumgullion Pass, Baldy Cinco
TH Summit Spring Creek Pass
SE 10,898'
TVG 2500'
RT 7.5 miles both peaks
STRENUOUS

The Colorado Trail, leading to the base of Baldy Cinco, departs across from the information site at the top of Spring Creek Pass and climbs just south of the Continental Divide to the top of Snow Mesa. Following this trail will lead you through both forest and open areas until just over 11,800' when the trees suddenly disappear and you will find yourself on a rocky trail climbing up to Snow Mesa. There are several cairns along the trail to Snow Mesa, with a particularly large one at the top. Once on top of Snow Mesa, there continue to be post cairns, but there really is no trail across the wide open tundra. It's a good idea to look behind you occasionally while crossing this tundra to note the location of the trail down to Spring Creek Pass, as the cairns on top are not very close together.

On the drive between Slumgullion Pass and Spring Creek Pass, there is a sign indicating a view area for 13,383', Baldy Cinco. Actually this suggested view area allows you see Baldy *no es* Cinco, a view which may prove confusing when you arrive at Snow Mesa. After using our map and dutifully planning our route before the hike, when we arrived at Snow Mesa, the route appeared to be obvious. We went a little lower than the trail markers, skirting around the top of the East Fork Cebolla Creek drainage, and climbed the mountain we had observed from Highway 149. On the top, while having lunch, Fr. Jim remarked that the next peak over really didn't look 200' lower, but we just continued eating lunch. Pretty soon, however, the height of the neighboring peak began to really bother us, so we made a careful study of the map, and sure enough, we had climbed the WRONG mountain. We were on top of 13,313' Baldy *no es* Cinco. This is the last hike and summit we shared with Cyr. He was really impressed with this mountain peak, saying it was good enough for him, and chose to wait on its summit with his dog, Friday, while Fr. Jim and I continued over to the proper Baldy Cinco.

If I were doing this again, I would do it exactly the same way, as the NW face of this first mountain is really spectacular, and we even saw two small herds of elk from the summit. In addition, the hike over to Baldy Cinco showed off some of the most beautiful wildflowers of the summer. High up at 13,000' we were especially rewarded with Parry's Primrose in a damp area. The Alpine Forget-Me-Nots were quite prolific as were the Siberian Smelowskia. I also saw Alpine Clover and lots of Moss Campion. It was very beautiful.

An alternate, although slightly longer route, to Baldy Cinco is up the Tumble Creek drainage with the entire hike in the La Garita Wilderness. See the Tumble Creek hike for directions.

Baldy Cinco from Baldy *no es* Cinco

POWDERHORN

The Ute Indians loved the lush grasslands of the Powderhorn area, and it was one of their favorite hunting grounds. After the Utes came the Spanish, followed by prospectors and trappers, but the first white settlers were those who, like the Utes, saw the value of the lush grasslands and used them for ranching. The Cebolla Creek Road (CR 27) passes these old ranches, many of which are still being ranched today. The name *Powderhorn* originates from the fact that, when viewed from a ridge above, the shape of the Powderhorn Valley resembles an old powderhorn. To reach Powderhorn from Gunnison, drive west from the last stoplight on Highway 50 for 8.7 miles to the Lake City bridge and intersection with Highway 149. Follow Highway 149 for 17.2 miles to the intersection with CR 27 and you will be in Powderhorn.

Trailheads and roads are the following distances from Powderhorn on CR 27.

Cathedral (Los Pinos Road) is 15.9 miles
FR 790 is 6.9 miles
Big Meadow/Cebolla Trail is 6.2 miles
Perfecto Creek (FR 794.2B) is 10 miles
FR 794 is 14.1 miles
Stewart Creek TH is 18.8 miles
Eddiesville TH is 19 miles
Powderhorn Park TH is 19.2 miles
Mineral Creek Road is 19.7 miles
Mineral Creek TH is 20.2 miles
Rough Creek TH is 20.9 miles
Brush Creek TH is 25.8 miles
Deer Lakes Campground (Devil's Lake) is 28.4 miles
Slumgullion Pass Road (149) is 31.1 miles

Trailheads and roads are the following distances from Powderhorn on Highway 149:

Indian Creek Road (CR 58) is 3.7 miles
Powderhorn Lakes TH is 10 miles

158

COCHETOPA

By 1863, the Ute Indians of the Colorado Territory had been moved to the Western Slope. The Treaty of 1868 required two Indian agencies to be established on the reservation. One of these agencies was located on the Cochetopa (Ute name meaning *pass of the buffalo*) and named the Los Pinos Indian Agency. Several peaks in the area are named in honor of the Ute Indians:

Mt. Ouray, 13,971'   Chief Ouray, Ute spokesman
Chipeta Mountain, 12,850' Wife of Chief Ouray
Mt. Antero, 14,269'   Chief Antero, Uintah band
Tabeguache Peak, 14,155' Tabeguache band
Mt. Shavano, 14,229' Chief Shavano

This vast area has seen ranching and logging, and both are still ongoing today. Many of the several roads on the Cochetopa are old, as well as, new logging roads. The original roads were the Los Pinos Pass, Old Cochetopa Pass and the Saguache and San Juan Toll Road. Crossing the Cochetopa from the east provides an alternative to the Los Pinos Road for arriving at Big Meadow, Stewart Creek and Eddiesville Trailheads. Drive east from Gunnison on Highway 50 for 7.7 miles to the intersection of Highway 114 and turn right. Follow Highway 114 for 20.3 miles to the sign indicating the Old Indian Agency (NN 14 RD). Turn right and go 7.0 miles past Dome Lakes to 15 GG RD. Turn right and go 4.0 miles to the Stewart Creek Road sign and bear right on FR 794.

The trailheads and roads of FR 794 are the following distances from this Stewart Creek sign:

Nutras Creek is 14.5 miles
Stewart Creek TH is 16.7 miles
Eddiesville TH is 17.0 miles

POWDERHORN PARK TRAIL

USGS Mineral Mountain
TH Cebolla Creek Road
SE 9000'
TVG 1760'
RT 10 miles Powderhorn Park
RT 12.6 miles Robbers Roost
MODERATE TO STRENUOUS

While driving south on Cebolla Creek Road (FR 788) towards Slumgullion Pass, the trailhead will be on the right immediately after crossing Mineral Creek. Initially the trail passes through private property and it is important to close all gates. The trail remains on private property until after the second gate. As the trail climbs gently out of the Cebolla Creek Valley, it passes through open country of sagebrush and grass. The view to the rear of the Mineral Creek drainage is spectacular and will be very enjoyable on the return from Powderhorn Park. There are many pretty wildflowers, particularly Indian Paintbrush, adding color to the grass. The trail contours around and above Wood Gulch, passing first through scattered Bristlecone Pines before entering cool forest. A little before Powderhorn Park, the trail will open up again, pass through a third gate, and finally climb up to the head of Wood Gulch and into the park. This park is quite expansive and of particular notice are the Shrubby Cinquefoil which grow abundantly on the margins of the park.

It is about five miles to the beginning of the park. Continuing on the right fork of the trail for another 1.3 miles to the north end of Powderhorn Park, will lead to an old cabin at Robber's Roost. This was an old cowcamp from the 1920's. Also, from the northern end of the park is a distant view of the rugged Elk Mountains combined with the East Fork drainage of Powderhorn Creek below. The highest elevation in the park is about 10,760'. It is also possible to continue on the left fork of the original trail for an additional 8 miles to Powderhorn Lakes.

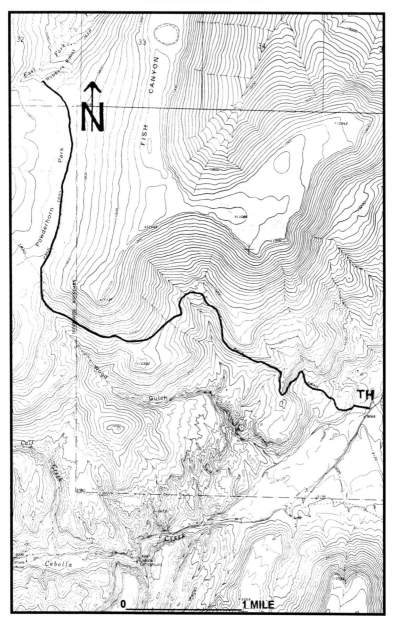

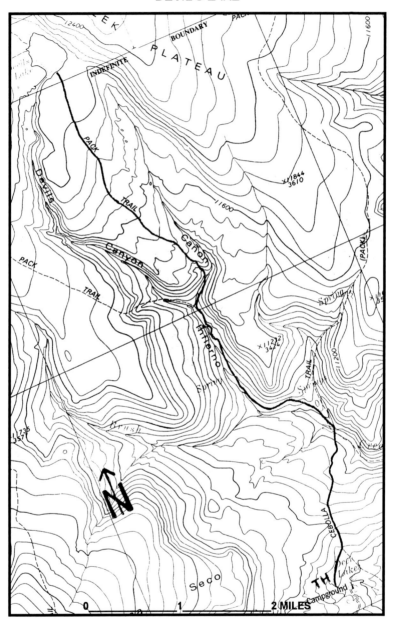

DEVIL'S LAKE 12,000'
USGS Cannibal Plateau
TH Cebolla Creek Road
SE 10,400' Deer Lakes Campground
TVG 2000' plus 500' return
RT 12 miles
STRENUOUS

This trail can be accessed from the Cebolla Creek Road (FR 788) at Brush Creek, or by going to the end of Deer Lakes Campground and following the cement walk to a trail leading to the trailhead. Either way, during the first three miles of the trail until the branch of Cañon Infierno and Devil's Canyon, you may encounter some trail bikes, as this portion of the trail only borders the La Garita Wilderness. Both trails require a big stream crossing at Brush Creek. If you choose to depart from Deer Lakes Campground, expect a vertical gain of 500' in less than a mile on your return over to the campground at the end of the hike.

It is a little over one mile after leaving Brush Creek and entering Cañon Infierno until the intersection with Devil's Canyon Trail. The intersection is well signed and you will take the trail to the right which climbs up out of Cañon Infierno. At the top of the canyon, head in a northwesterly direction until you come to a huge sea of willows. Begin looking for a tall trail post on your right. At this point, there is not much, if any, trail, but Devil's Lake is north of you. Look at the ridge to the north across these vast willows and find the largest patch without willows near the top of the ridge. Head for that spot. This will require some interesting maze work while battling the wonderful willows on assorted elk and people trails. As you get nearer to the bare patch, another tall trail marker (with 3 skulls on it) will be visible. After the skull marker, and a little further up, the lake will be north of you, even though the feeling is that it should be more northwest. It is right up against the far end of Calf Creek Plateau which spans the horizon to the north and east. It is a slight drop down from 12,000' to Devil's Lake.

POWDERHORN & THE COCHETOPA

At the south end of the lake is an old windmill. This was put in as an experiment to pump oxygen into the lake in an effort to prevent winter kill of the fish. The lake, however, continues to lose its fish over the winter. When there are fish, expect to find Brook Trout and Cutthroat.

Walk west for a view into Devil's Canyon, before returning to the original trail and the wonderful willows. There are many nice camping spots while still in the protection of the timber, just before the willows, if you want to make this a camping trip. Cañon Infierno is filled with aspen trees and is beautiful as a fall hike.

Top Photo: Boy Scouts at the skull marker
Bottom photo: Devil's Lake with Calf Creek Plateau on the right

POWDERHORN LAKES
USGS Powderhorn Lakes
TH Indian Creek Road
SE 11,000'
TVG 860' to Upper Lake
RT 8 miles Powderhorn Lakes
MODERATE
TVG 1600' to Calf Creek Plateau
TVG 600' Devil's Lake to Calf Creek Plateau
RT 12 miles Devil's Lake
STRENUOUS

The Indian Creek Road is located along Highway 149 towards Lake City about 4 miles beyond Powderhorn. The road is signed only with CR 58. Following this road for about 10 miles to its end will bring you to the Powderhorn Lakes Trailhead. The trail to the lakes is all on BLM land in the Powderhorn Wilderness and very well maintained. The hike to the lakes is relatively easy, passing through timber, into a spacious open park, and then back into the timber until just before reaching the lower lake. At the open park the talus which is in view is on the east end of the large cirque which surrounds the upper lake towards the south. The top of this cirque continues to form Calf Creek Plateau. There were many Plumed Avens in the open parks, and in the trees by the lower lake, I found several clumps of Jacob's Ladder. All along the trail Sky Pilots were quite common.

Sky Pilots

The trail from the lower lake to the upper lake seems to disappear just a bit before reaching the upper lake. Head over towards the talus and you can't miss the lake. Powderhorn Lakes support Snake River Cutthroat, Rainbow and Brook Trout. These lakes provide a scenic spot for a camping and fishing trip.

To climb up onto Calf Creek Plateau, either for the view or to go over to Devil's Lake, head north from the upper lake until you find a trail up the grassy slope leading to the ridge. From the top of the ridge, work your way back towards the south and the other side of Calf Creek Plateau. You should be able to pick up the trail to descend to Devil's Lake after about a mile of walking on the plateau. At the very least, I would recommend hiking up the grassy slope part way for a stunning view of both lakes. On your return trip, you will discover that there was a lot of gentle up and down on the Powderhorn Lakes Trail.

Upper Powderhorn Lake from the ridge leading to Calf Creek Plateau

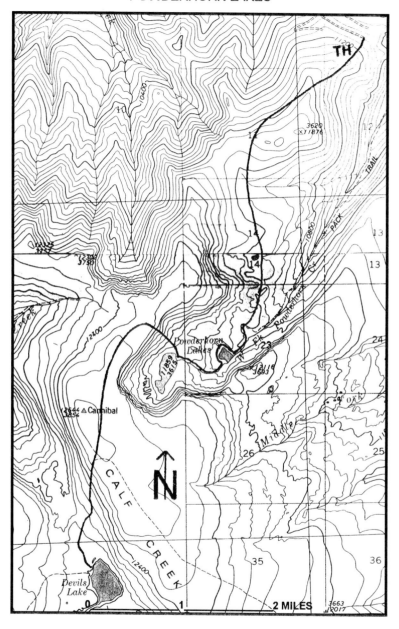

BALDY CHATO 13,401'
USGS Stewart Peak
TH Big Meadow Park
SE 11,500'
TVG 1900'
RT 4 miles
MODERATE TO STRENUOUS

The Cebolla Trail leaves FR 790 at Big Meadow where E Pinos Creek culverts under the road. This is slightly different than what is shown on the USGS map, as it does not show the continuation of FR 790 to Groundhog Park and Los Pinos Pass. However, the trailhead is well signed and easy to locate on FR 790. Follow the Cebolla Trail at least through the trees to the beginning of the willows. Once at the willows, you may be able to spot a route through them, but I can recommend staying on the trail, marked by tall posts, until you are beyond the willows. Next, simply head south for about 1 mile on the gentle slopes of 13,401' Baldy Chato (Spanish for *flat-faced*) until you come to the summit. After this gentle climb, the steep west face, falling directly off the summit, is really impressive, as is the view across the Spring Creek drainage. If you were to follow the ridge south and then east you would come to 13,983', Stewart Peak. This would make a wonderful continuation of the hike on a day that weather would permit the additional 1.75 miles of high altitude ridge walking and climbing.

I would recommend (from experience) not taking any chances with the weather, even if climbing a gentle peak like Baldy Chato, as it can be very difficult to find your way back in a whiteout. My time would have been better spent playing with my compass instead of my camera when Fr. Jim, Cyr and I were watching the approach of a huge storm on July 3, 1995. Luckily, we had taken a compass reading on the way up, and that proved indispensable on the way back as we returned in a raging blizzard which left about 3 inches of new snow. We were unable to relocate the Cebolla Trail, quite visible, however, during photography of the approaching storm, but we did finally find our way back to the jeep with the use of map, compass and altimeter. The three of us and Cyr's little dog, Friday, were totally caked with snow at the end of this "summer?" hike!

THE STORM

View of Spring Creek drainage from the summit of Baldy Chato

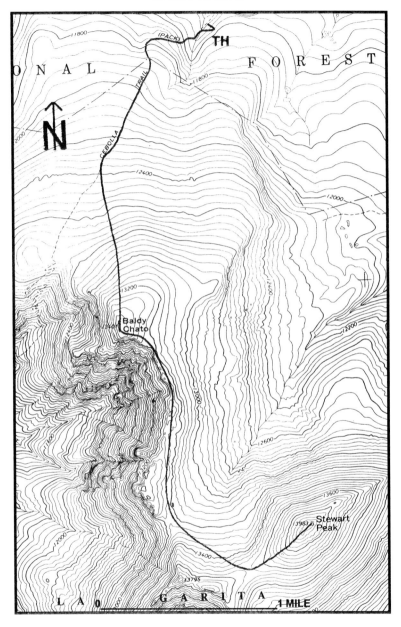

BALDY ALTO

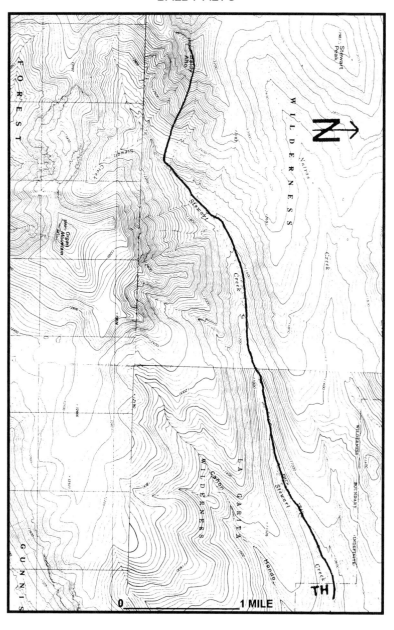

BALDY ALTO 13,698'
USGS Elk Park, Stewart Peak, San Luis Peak
TH Stewart Creek
SE 10,400'
TVG 3300'
RT 10 miles
VERY STRENUOUS

Baldy Alto, 13,698', can be climbed from the Stewart Creek Trail, either singly or after a climb of San Luis Peak. After leaving the trailhead, follow the trail which climbs gently for about four miles up along Stewart Creek. There are two stream crossings with logs which can be negotiated during runoff, although the water may be sloshing the logs later in the day. When you break out of the timber, the ridge leading to Baldy Alto will be on your right and the summit will be ahead of you. Just hike off across the tundra to gain the ridge and follow it to the summit. Return by the same route.

Ruth Bains on San Luis Peak with Stewart Peak and Baldy Alto behind

POWDERHORN & THE COCHETOPA

    If climbing Baldy Alto after San Luis Peak, contour around behind the rocky knob above the saddle between San Luis and Organ Mountain, and then follow the ridges up, down and over to Baldy Alto. The last ridge to the summit is steep and loose, so take care. Enjoy the wonderful Alpine Forget-Me Nots while up on the high ridges. If you have approached Baldy Alto from San Luis, on the return continue NE from the summit down along the ridge until you can drop safely into the Stewart Creek drainage without having to negotiate any cliffs. It is easy to find a route, and the Stewart Creek Valley is always in view.

    I particularly enjoyed taking this hike with my son, Ben, his friend Steven Wells, and Steven's grandmother, Ruth McDonough Bains. Both Ruth and her late husband, Bill McDonough, grew up on ranches on the Cochetopa and the Powderhorn Valley.

Baldy Alto and San Luis Peak from Stewart Peak

STEWART PEAK 13,983'

USGS Elk Park, Stewart Peak
TH Nutras Creek
SE 11,000'
TVG 3000'
RT 8 miles
STRENUOUS

The trailhead at Nutras Creek is not an official trailhead, and therefore, there are no signs other than the little sign which names the creek. Pull off the Stewart Creek Road (FR 794) and park along the little road leading to an informal camping area. For approximately 2.5 miles, there is a fairly distinct, gentle trail. This trail will take you into a side drainage of Nutras Creek and then fizzle out in the willows. This is the way we went, and I think this side drainage is a good approach to the peak, as the main drainage looks like a real bushwhack. Follow the side drainage, keeping the willows on your right, until the forest on your left thins out. At this point, turn left and climb to the top of the ridge which is separating you from the main Nutras Creek drainage. Follow the ridge west until you can get on the big ridge coming from Stewart Peak. I recommend staying on the ridge of Stewart, as the face is a little loose and tiresome.

Stewart Peak (left) and Baldy Chato (right)

On the summit there is an incredible view of the surrounding peaks and valleys. This wonderful peak is only 17' short of 14,000'! After visiting the summit of Stewart, you can continue on a traverse of the summit and descend to a saddle between Stewart and 13,795' Unnamed Peak. From this saddle either the Unnamed Peak may be climbed, or you can go over a knob and climb Baldy Alto. If either of these peaks are climbed, it would be best to bushwhack down the main drainage of Nutras Creek to return to the car. I would recommend taking a map and compass for the climb of Stewart Peak as the drainages are a little confusing.

Ptarmigan hiking up Stewart Peak

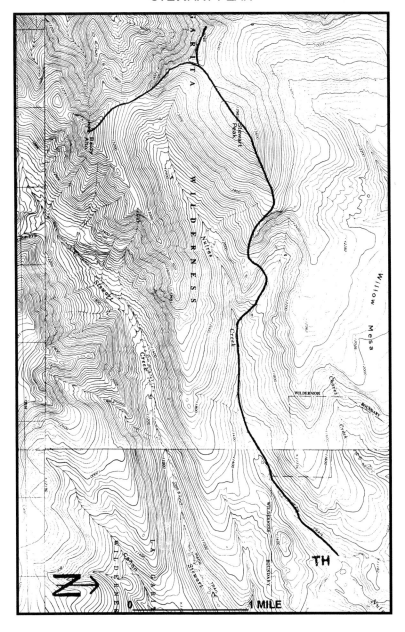

CAÑON DIABLO
USGS Elk Park, Halfmoon Pass
TH Eddiesville
SE 10,320'
TVG 1400'
RT 10 miles
MODERATE

For the first 3 miles beyond the Eddiesville Trailhead along the Skyline Trail, there is an elevation gain of only 400', making this a very easy stroll to the Cañon Diablo Trail and also a nice hike for children. A major portion of these first three miles is in open meadow with beautiful wildflowers and some extraordinary beaver work. The rest of the time the trail is in the woods. Of particular notice in the woods are the Bristlecone Pine trees. Just before the unmarked Diablo Trail, the trail has two switchbacks as it climbs around, and above, a small, picturesque canyon in a wooded area. When the valley once again opens, the intersection with the trail to Cañon Diablo is immediately to the left. The trail is a bit faint, but can be followed over to the stream crossing. Later in the hiking season, you can expect to find some logs across Cochetopa Creek.

Becca McCormick & Sarah Garcia crossing Cochetopa Cr. to Cañon Diablo

Once on the trail to Cañon Diablo, you enter a remote, wild place. Although the deadfall has been cleared in years past, there are now several logs across the trail. It is still an easy trail to follow as it winds through both woods, and near willows, up to the head of the canyon. After the first climb up into the woods, be sure to turn around and see Organ Mountain across the Cochetopa Valley. It is sometimes possible to encounter Bighorn Sheep at the head of Cañon Diablo. I can recommend this hike for either an all day hike or an easy backpack, as water is always close by. Cochetopa Creek supports Rainbow, Brown, Brookies, and Colorado River Cutthroat Trout.

ORGAN MOUNTAIN 13,801'

USGS Elk Park, Halfmoon Pass, San Luis Peak
TH Eddiesville
SE 10,320'
TVG 3500'
RT 12 miles
VERY STRENUOUS

Beginning at the Eddiesville Trailhead, hike up Cochetopa Creek on the Skyline Trail. The Cañon Diablo Trail is reached in about 3 miles. Continue on the main trail, past this junction for approximately 1.5 miles. Hiking much further than 1.5 miles will bring you into the cliff areas of Organ Mountain. The trail has been passing under the easternmost flanks of Organ Mountain on your right for quite some time, and it is now time to pick a place and head for treeline. Once at treeline, it is easy to follow the grassy slopes for another mile up to the summit of 13,801', Organ Mountain. You will have a view of both the Cochetopa Creek and Stewart Creek drainages, as well as all the surrounding peaks. There are some really impressive cliffs down the south face. Return by the same route.

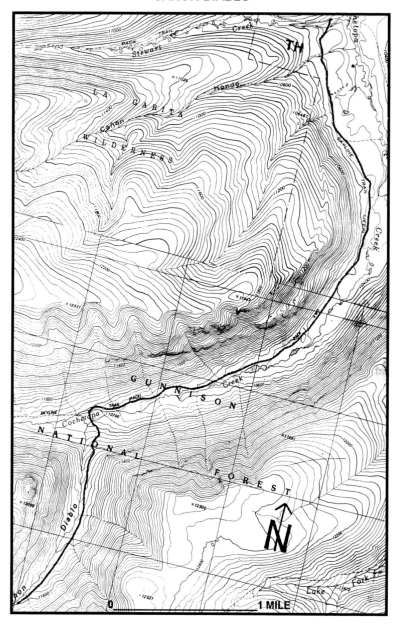

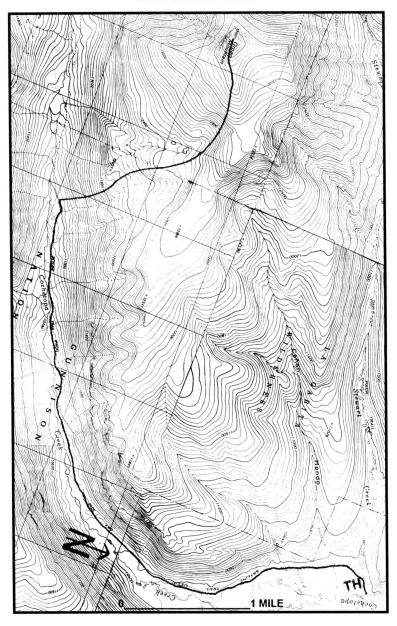

STEWART CREEK / COCHETOPA CREEK
USGS Elk Park, Stewart Peak, San Luis Peak, Halfmoon Pass
TH Stewart Creek
SE 10,400'
TVG 2700'
RT 12.5 miles
STRENUOUS

This is a nice backpacking trip or a long day hike, making a loop between Stewart Creek and Cochetopa Creek. Begin by hiking up Stewart Creek on the well-defined Stewart Creek Trail. For a backpacking trip, plan to camp on the first day before leaving the trees near Baldy Alto. The second day continue up the drainage and follow the cairns to the saddle at 13,107' between San Luis Peak and Organ Mountain. Take plenty of time to enjoy the high tundra flowers, especially the Alpine Forget-Me-Nots. The view of Baldy Alto, San Luis and Organ Mountains are beautiful. Continue down into the Cochetopa Creek drainage and join the Skyline Trail heading east. Find a place to camp when again in the trees. On the third day, take an easy walk out to the Eddiesville Trailhead, enjoying the wildflowers and Bristlecone Pines. From Eddiesville Trailhead, walk the additional .2 miles along the road back to the Stewart Creek Trailhead. This circle trip would be an excellent choice for those who wish to fish, as these two creeks support Brookies, Browns and Colorado River Cutthroat. Cochetopa Creek also has Rainbow Trout.

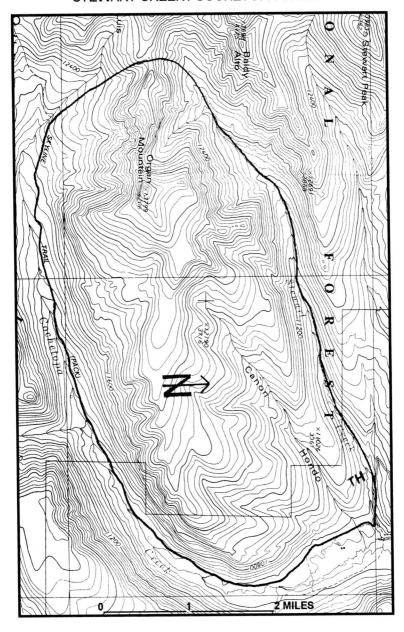

QUARTZ CREEK VALLEY
PARLIN

To reach the Quartz Creek Valley from Gunnison, take Highway 50 east from McDonalds for 11.2 miles to Parlin, a small settlement named for early pioneer, John T. Parlin. Parlin's son and train engineer, Frank Parlin, was killed when his train went out of control and crashed on the east side of Marshall Pass in 1909.

Trailheads and roads are the following distances from Parlin on CR 76 and FR 765:

Ohio City is 8.7 miles
Pitkin (City Hall) is 15.3 miles
Tin Cup is 35.1 miles

OHIO CITY

The Gold Creek Road turns north (left) on FR 771 at Ohio City. Gold Creek was originally named Ohio Creek because so many of the members of the early prospecting party of Fred Lottis were from Ohio. Since there were several very profitable gold mines up this valley, the name of the creek was changed to Gold Creek. Ohio City was named after the original Ohio Creek and retained its name. The remains of some of these mines can be seen on the drive to Gold Creek Campground.

Trailheads and roads on the Gold Creek Road are the following distances from Ohio City:

Gold Creek Campground is 7 miles
Mill Lake TH is 7 miles
Lamphier Lakes TH is 7.1 miles
New Dollar Gulch Road is 8.2 miles
Gold Creek Trail is 8.5 miles

PITKIN

The town of Pitkin was originally called Quartzville for the quartz which could be found in the area. It soon became Pitkin, renamed for Colorado Governor, Frederick W. Pitkin. The lure of silver, along with the finding of valuable silver in four mines in the area, caused the population of the town of Pitkin to swell to 4000 people in August of 1881. However, shallow veins of silver, silver panics and fires all contributed to the demise of Pitkin as a major mining town. Over the years it has relied on a small lumber industry, the state fish hatchery and the real estate market for its survival as a tiny mountain town.

Trailheads and roads continuing on FR 765 are the following distances from Pitkin:

Alpine Tunnel Road is 3.1 miles

Summit of Cumberland Pass is 11.3 miles

Tin Cup is 19.8 miles (46.3 miles from Gunnison)

TIN CUP

The small summer town of Tin Cup got its name when an early prospector, Ben Gray, filled his tin cup with creek water for a drink and saw a gold color in the cup. With "gold" having been discovered in a tin cup, the settlement ultimately was called "Tin Cup". The town boomed during the gold mining era with the heaviest producing mine being the Gold Cup Mine. Like most of the "boom towns" of the gold rush, Tin Cup slowly faded away. Today it is a pleasant summer community, with several of the original buildings restored and useable.

Trailheads and roads on FR 765 are the following distances from Tin Cup:

Mirror Lake Road (FR 267) is in Tin Cup

Mt. Kreutzer TH is 2.1 miles

Taylor Reservoir is 7.9 miles

Gunnison is 40.5 miles

UPPER LAMPHIER LAKE 11,700'
GUNSIGHT PASS 12,167'
BRONCHO MOUNTAIN 12,834'

USGS Fairview Peak
TH Gold Creek Campground
SE 10,030'
TVG 1,670' to Upper Lamphier Lake
RT 6 miles
MODERATE
TVG 2140' to Gunsight Pass
RT 8 miles
MODERATE TO STRENUOUS
TVG 2800' to Broncho Mountain
RT 10 miles
STRENUOUS

The Lamphier Lakes Trailhead is .1 mile beyond Gold Creek Campground just after crossing the Lamphier Creek bridge. This hike would also make a fine beginning backpack for kids, providing them with the opportunity to reach a beautiful high lake without too much distance. Lamphier Lake provides some good fishing for Snake River Cutthroat Trout. The climb is gentle most of the way, with a few switchbacks on the upper portion. From Upper Lamphier Lake, hike an additional mile up to 12,176', Gunsight Pass on the trail found at the NE side of the lake. It is also possible to climb another mile to 12,834', Broncho Mountain by following the ridges up to the east of the summit of the pass. 12,985', Squaretop Mountain, bordering Lamphier Lake on the west, can be climbed with careful route finding through large boulders, and steep loose rock.

Gunsight Pass --Photo by Nancy Ruehle

MILL LAKE 11,480'
FOSSIL MOUNTAIN 12,749'
SQUARETOP MOUNTAIN 12,985'
HENRY MOUNTAIN 13,254'

USGS Fairview Peak

TH Gold Creek Campground

SE 10,030'

TVG 1450' to Mill Lake

RT 5 miles Mill Lake

MODERATE

TVG 2720' to Fossil Mountain

TVG 3000' to Squaretop Mountain

TVG 3500' to Henry Mountain

RT 10.25 miles Henry Mountain Circle

VERY STRENUOUS

Boulder Lake Trail and Mill Lake Trail share the same path for about .5 mile until the wilderness boundary, so it is possible to encounter trail bikes until there. From the boundary, where the trails separate, the Mill Lake Trail climbs gently NE for awhile through an old growth spruce and fir forest. Hiking through these trees gives the sensation of being miles from civilization in a very deep forest. Perhaps this is due to the long, hairy, epiphytic (non parasitic) moss which is hanging from the trees. This old forest also provides habitat for some uncommon plants, critters and birds. Although not steep or long, the portion of the trail from about 10,500' to 10,900' contains 12 switchbacks. The last part of the trail straightens out again for the final push to the lake. The entire hike is in beautiful forest, and the lake is in a gorgeous setting just under Fossil Mountain. A great day can be spent at Mill Lake fishing for Snake River Cutthroat Trout.

If you wish to climb a peak or two, hike around the lake to the north (right) until you are below the ridge which leads to Fossil Mountain, the beautiful peak at the head of the lake.

Traverse back slightly NE to assume the ridge, thus avoiding cliffs and loose rock. It is now a nice ridge walk around to the west and the summit of Fossil Mountain at 12,749'. As long as you are up there, consider going over to 12,985', Squaretop Mountain and 13,254', Henry Mountain which lie slightly north west from Fossil Mountain. When we did it, we bypassed Squaretop on the way to Henry, then climbed it on the way back, and finally dropped down to Lamphier Lake, making a nice circle trip. It did require some careful route finding on the way down to Lamphier Lake from the north side of Squaretop.

Boy Scouts on Gunsight Pass

It is also possible to visit Boulder Lake from Mill Lake. While facing the lake at the outlet, look for the easy way to climb to the saddle between Fossil Mountain and Sheep Mountain. Hike around the lake as far as needed before heading up to the saddle. Once on the saddle, you can quite easily drop down to Boulder Lake. Sheep Mountain is also easy to climb from this saddle. Remember that if you choose to return via the Boulder Lake Trail, you will probably be sharing it with trail bikes, as it is a popular route.

MILL & LAMPHIER LAKES -- TRAILS, PEAKS & PASS

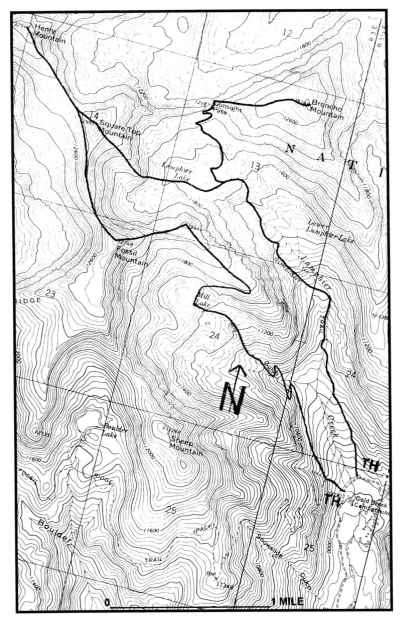

FAIRVIEW PEAK 13,214'
USGS Fairview Peak
TH Gold Creek Campground
SE 10,030'
TVG 3200'
RT 11 miles Gold Creek
STRENUOUS
TH Summit Cumberland Pass
SE 12,015'
TVG 1220'
RT 6 miles Cumberland Pass
MODERATE

13,214', Fairview Peak can be climbed from Gold Creek Campground. Hike 1.4 miles on the jeep road, passing the Lamphier Lakes Trailhead, until you come to the jeep road leading to New Dollar Gulch. Hike this road for about 2.25 miles until you are below the saddle between Terrible Mountain and Fairview Peak at about 11,000'. Head up to the saddle and pick up the trail which leads to Fairview. This peak is really worth visiting as it does have a "fair" view.

Near the summit of Fairview Peak --Photo by Fr. Jim Koenigsfeld

QUARTZ CREEK VALLEY

There was a lot of mining activity on Terrible Mountain, and it is important to look out for some huge mine shafts which go straight down for a long ways. Be careful with kids! Needless to say, if you do have access to 4-wheel drive, a little over 6 miles could be shaved off the climb to Fairview Peak.

Fairview Peak from Cumberland Pass

Another shorter way to climb Fairview Peak is to drive to the top of Cumberland Pass and then hike west over Green Mountain and up along the high ridges for about 3 miles to Fairview Peak. The little building on top of Fairview Peak can be seen from the summit of Cumberland Pass. This trip would definitely require favorable weather due to the exposed, high elevation.

FAIRVIEW PEAK

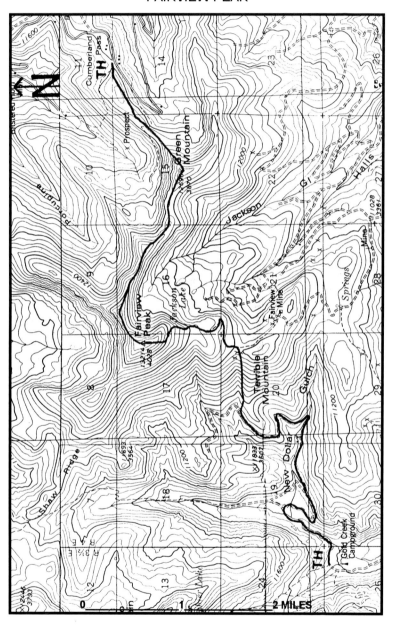

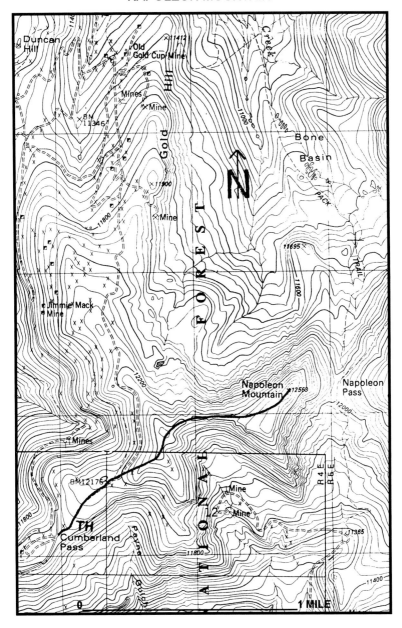

NAPOLEON MOUNTAIN 12,563'
USGS Cumberland Pass
TH Summit Cumberland Pass
SE 12,015'
TVG 550'
RT 2.6 miles
MODERATE

This is definitely not a wilderness hike, as some people choose to drive their off-road vehicles on much of the terrain near the summit of Cumberland Pass. I am including it in this book because it provides a chance to hike at high altitude without a long approach or a 4-wheel drive vehicle. The summit of Napoleon Mountain can not be seen from the summit of Cumberland Pass. Hike to the northeast via assorted roads to the highest visible spot. From this high spot, you will be able to see the Middle Willow Creek drainage where Tin Cup's famous Gold Cup Mine was located. Continue by following the ridge over to what looks like a big pile of rocks--Napoleon Mountain. This ridge walk is great for seeing some of the flowers of the high alpine tundra.

Anne Ash on the summit of Napoleon Mountain with Taylor Park behind

From the summit, you can look down to Napoleon Pass, which was the chief wagon route to take the ore from the Gold Cup Mine to the Quartz Creek Valley. Looking across Napoleon Pass, you will see Fitzpatrick Peak which sits on the Continental Divide. Both Mt. Kreutzer and Emma Burr Mountain are easy to see, also. I think the most spectacular view was down Middle Willow Creek to Tincup and beyond to Taylor Park.

Looking down on Napoleon Pass from Napoleon Mountain

FITZPATRICK PEAK 13,112'
USGS Cumberland Pass
TH Cumberland Pass Road
SE 10,695'
TVG 2420'
RT 4.4 miles steep route
STRENUOUS
RT 6.4 miles gentle route
MODERATE TO STRENUOUS

Fitzpatrick Peak is another peak with a relatively short, multiuse approach up to the summit of Napoleon Pass. Park on Cumberland Pass Road just before the road takes a major curve to the left. Follow the rough jeep road which has been washed out by the creek and it will run into another road from further down on the Cumberland Pass Road. After one switchback, the road goes in a northerly direction. Do not take the first turn to the right which heads east to Graphite Basin. In approximately one mile, the main road will curve to the west, and the Napoleon Pass Trail will continue north. Follow this "many track" trail to the summit of Napoleon Pass at 12,000'.

The short, steep route up Fitzpatrick is to head due east from the summit of the pass. Try to stay on the grassy slopes until the summit cone, as the rocky slopes on Fitzpatrick are really loose. It is not bad working up through the rocks leading to the summit. From the summit you will be able to look down into the Chalk Creek Valley, and also see Tin Cup Pass joining St. Elmo and Tin Cup. Sleighs pulled by mules carried passengers over Tin Cup Pass during the winter months in the 1880's. Today it is a jeep road. Napoleon Mountain just looked like a small pile of rocks when climbed from Cumberland Pass, but from Fitzpatrick Peak, it looks like a mountain.

If the direct route up Fitzpatrick is too steep, stay on Napoleon Pass Trail until a fork to the right with a trail which traverses upward across the side of Fitzpatrick. Follow this trail for a little less than a mile and then climb the gentle ridge along the Continental Divide up to the summit of the peak.

Fitzpatrick Peak from Napoleon Mountain

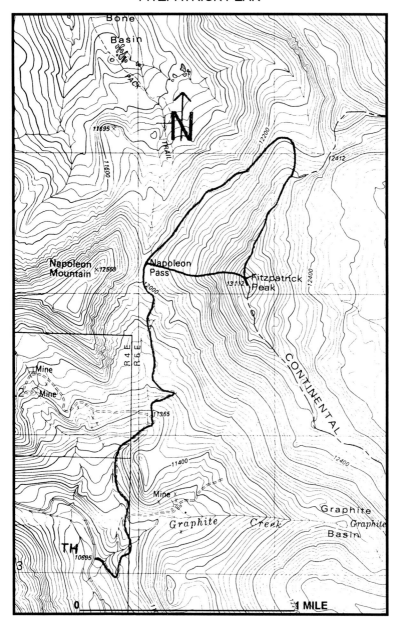

ALPINE TUNNEL
ALTMAN PASS 11,960'

USGS Cumberland Pass
TH End of Alpine Tunnel Road
SE 11,460'
TVG 150' West Portal
RT .5 mile
EASY
TVG 1150' Altman Pass and East Portal
RT 2.5 miles
MODERATE

The first passenger train through the Alpine Tunnel arrived in Pitkin on July 13, 1882. Although the Denver South Park and Pacific Railroad lost the race with the Rio Grande Railroad to lay tracks to Gunnison, the Alpine Tunnel will always remain an historic marvel in the Quartz Creek Valley. The railroad fare from Denver to Gunnison via the Alpine Tunnel was $15.00. Drive from Pitkin for three miles on FR 765 to the start of the Alpine Tunnel railroad grade. Turn right and follow this historic grade for ten miles to a parking area just below the little Alpine Station building near the West Portal of the tunnel.

Bernard Lebow by the old stone engine house --Photo by Susan Lebow

QUARTZ CREEK VALLEY

The shortest hike is from the parking area to the West Portal of the tunnel. You will notice some ongoing historical preservation and renovation. Hopefully, some time in the near future, after the rubble is removed, we will be able to look inside the tunnel and see the marvelous construction that allowed a train to pass under the Continental Divide. Until then, all that is visible are the remains of the snow shed and a pile of rocks and dirt where the train entered the tunnel. None the less, you will have a feeling of the past when hiking past the remains of the beautiful stone engine house and several fallen buildings on the way to the portal. The little Alpine Station has been restored and provides a nice visitor center.

Remains of the old snow shed near the West Portal --Photo by Susan Lebow

This hike can be continued further by taking the trail over to the East Portal. The trail, although steep, is only about .5 mile long and goes over the Continental Divide via 11,940', Altman Pass. After the construction of the tunnel, Altman Pass, originally named for early explorer, Judge Henry Altman, was often referred to as Alpine Pass. The top of Altman Pass offers a chance to see many of Colorado's beautiful wildflowers growing in the high tundra.

WILLIAMS PASS 11,766'
MOUNT POOR 12,442'
ALPINE TUNNEL CIRCLE TRIP

USGS Cumberland Pass

TH Alpine Tunnel Road

SE 11,360'

TVG 400' Williams Pass

RT 2.5 miles

MODERATE

TVG 1100' Mount Poor

RT 4 miles

MODERATE

TVG 1250' Circle Trip

RT 8.5 miles

MODERATE

About 8 miles up the Alpine Tunnel Road, the trail to Williams Pass leaves just above the first section of the Palisades. The Palisades are the incredible rockwork that was done by hand in order to shore up the railroad grade. There is a vehicle pull-out and place to turn around just beyond the start of the trail. The old Alpine and South Park Toll Road once joined the Quartz Creek Valley with the settlement of Hancock via 11,766' Williams Pass, and the trail you will be following is the top portion of this old road. The toll road was in existence before the construction of the tunnel and its lower portions can be faintly seen below the Palisades. The trail climbs gradually for 1.25 miles to the summit of the pass and Colorado Columbine are abundant along this route through mid July. 12,442', Mount Poor separates Williams Pass from Altman Pass, and can easily be climbed from Williams Pass with an additional .75 mile hiking.

For another variation of this hike, continue down the far side of Williams Pass for 2 more miles until it intersects the railroad grade leading to the East Portal. You can then follow this grade for 3 miles up Tunnel Gulch to the East Portal, climb over the top to the West Portal via Altman Pass, and return to your car by hiking down the railroad grade past the old Alpine Station. From the intersection of Williams Pass and the railroad grade in Tunnel Gulch, you might find it interesting to take the short walk down to the old settlement of Hancock before hiking up to the East Portal.

Friends in front of the snow covered rubble of the East Portal

ALPINE TUNNEL, WILLIAMS PASS & MT. POOR

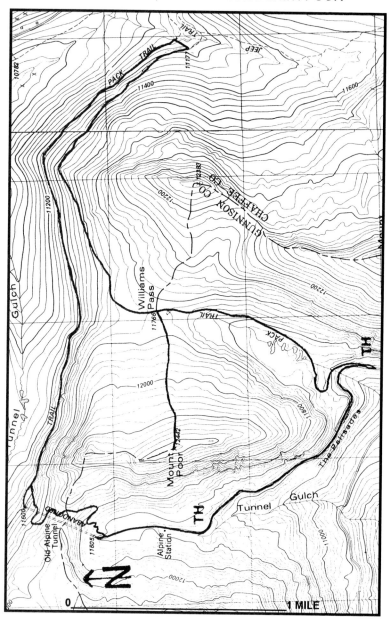

MT. KREUTZER & EMMA BURR MOUNTAIN

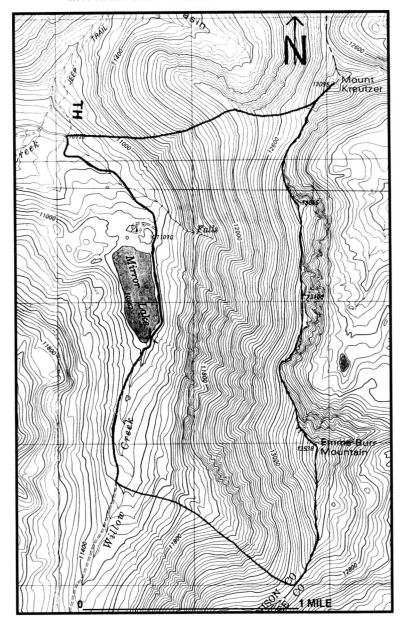

MOUNT KREUTZER 13095'
EMMA BURR MOUNTAIN 13,538'

USGS Cumberland Pass, Tin Cup
TH Mirror Lake Road
SE 10,720'
TVG 2375' Mount Kreutzer
RT 3 miles
STRENUOUS
TVG 3150' both peaks
RT 6 miles
STRENUOUS

Drive 2.1 miles from Tin Cup on the Mirror Lake Road and park at an area on the left which contains an outhouse and a sign for the Timberline Trail. Begin your climb to Mt. Kreutzer by heading east up the steep slope through the timber until you break out at about 12,000'. If you prefer to climb talus rather than bushwhacking in the timber, begin your climb a little bit closer towards Mirror Lake. Both ways will take you to the same ridge. When we were climbing in the timber, we discovered a tiny little ground nest which contained three baby birds with wide-open beaks. The tiny nest was hidden under some Kinnikinnik, and we were careful not to disturb the nest or the babies so that the mother bird would return.

QUARTZ CREEK VALLEY

When out of the timber, you will be able to spot 13,095', Mt. Kreutzer at the end of a long ridge to the east. Mt. Kreutzer was named for William Kreutzer, who was the first United States Forest Ranger assigned to the Gunnison National Forest. From the top of Mt. Kreutzer, you may choose to follow the ridge at 13,000' for 1.8 more miles along the top of the Continental Divide over to 13,538', Emma Burr Mountain. The view down the east side of this ridge is awesome, with many abrupt, long dropoffs. In addition, the flowers in this high alpine tundra are stunning!! We saw a virtual carpet of Alpine Avens, Alpine Forget-Me-Nots (my favorite), Fairy Primrose, and Alpine Spring Beauty. We also took time to smell the flowers and discovered it was the Forget-Me-Nots and Spring Beauties with the wonderful fragrance. Remember that it is very important to attempt this traverse only if the weather is free of thunderstorms.

On the ridge walk to Emma Burr Mountain

Emma Burr Mountain

From the summit of either Mt. Kreutzer or Emma Burr Mountain, it is easy to pick out several 14,000' peaks in the Collegiate Wilderness. Yale, Harvard, Columbia, Princeton, and Antero are the easiest to identify. Below the Divide on the west is Mirror Lake, which might provide a nice spot for family members not wishing to climb the mountains. Mirror Lake contains Rainbow Trout and Brookies for fishing. The road leading on up the high valley beyond Mirror Lake goes to Tin Cup Pass which was once the major wagon route over the Continental Divide between St. Elmo and Tin Cup. The easiest descent off of Emma Burr Mountain is to follow the ridge a little bit further south and then drop down to the Tin Cup Pass Road. Of course, it is possible to head more directly down to Mirror Lake, but the talus is steep and not particularly stable.

TAYLOR CANYON

The drive through beautiful Taylor Canyon follows the Taylor River all the way to a great park which the Utes referred to as *The Valley of the Gods*. In 1937, the work was completed in Taylor Park to create the existing reservoir and dam. Even with these additions, the desolate beauty of this high mountain park remains. Jim Taylor was the first prospector to really take notice of the park when he came to the Gunnison country searching for gold in 1860, after following a party of Ute Indians over the Continental Divide. The park, river and canyon are all named for Jim Taylor. Lottis Creek is named for Fred Lottis, another early prospector of the Taylor Park and Quartz Creek regions. To reach Taylor Canyon, drive 10 miles north from Gunnison on Highway 135 to the intersection with the paved Taylor Canyon Road (CR 742) which begins at Almont. Big Horn Sheep are often spotted from Taylor Canyon Road.

The trailheads and locations are the following distances from Almont on CR 742:

Gunnison Mountain Park is 3.2 miles
Summerville TH is 13.1 miles
South Lottis Creek TH is 16.7 miles
Taylor Reservoir is 23.2 miles
Tin Cup via FR 765 is 31.1 miles
Mirror Lake Road (FR 267) is 31.1 miles
Mt. Kreutzer TH is 2.1 miles

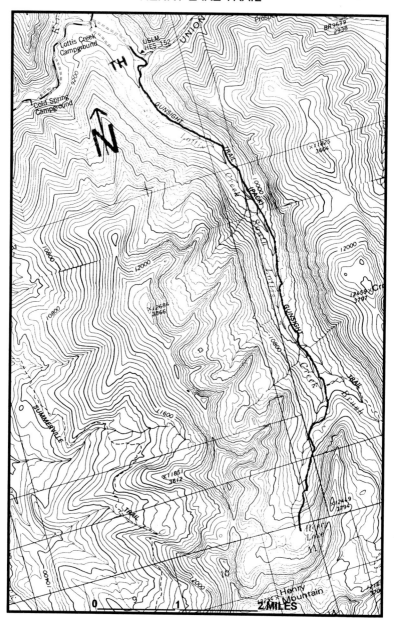

HENRY LAKE 11,704'
USGS Fairview Peak, Taylor Park Reservoir
TH Lottis Creek Campground
SE 9100'
TVG 2600'
RT 13 miles
STRENUOUS

The trailhead for Henry Lake is found at the second (east) entrance of the Lottis Creek Campground located on the Taylor Canyon Road. From the main road, drive through the campground to the south side and follow a small dirt road for .4 mile to the South Lottis Creek Trailhead. Once on the trail and after a very short distance, a trail leading to Union Park will branch off to the left. Stay right on the South Lottis Creek Trail. The trail will first pass through a pine and aspen forest in a wide valley. There are occasional open meadows as the trail leads very gently upwards into the spruce and fir. In the fall, the Parry's Gentian were very beautiful and abundant on this hike. The trail becomes quite rocky higher up into the valley.

Henry Mountain (l) above Henry Lake --Photo by Patrick Wells

After approximately 4.5 miles there will be a trail junction, with the left fork continuing to Gunsight Pass and over to Gold Creek, and the right fork leading to Henry Lake in two more miles. The trail steepens a little bit on the climb up to the lake, although it is still a very reasonable grade. I would recommend a visit to Henry Lake at 11,704', as a wonderful place for a backpacking trip, allowing time for camping, fishing for Snake River and Yellowstone Cutthroat Trout, and the possibility of climbing 13,254', Henry Mountain. The peak is often visible from the South Lottis Creek Trail, and being taller than its nearby neighbors, allows a fine view in all directions from its summit.

SUMMERVILLE TRAIL

USGS Matchless Mountain, Crystal Creek

TH Taylor Canyon Road

SE 8800'

TVG 2000'

RT 9 miles

MODERATE TO STRENUOUS

If you like solitude in the forest, I can certainly recommend this trail. The entire trail is 11 miles long and joins Taylor Canyon with the Fossil Ridge Trail. The description here will be the first 4.5 miles of the trail. The small Summerville Creek is criss-crossed by the trail six times in the first 1.5 miles. This little creek has been known to contain Colorado River Cutthroat and Brookies. The crossings are easy to splash through, but also have funky little log crossing bridges. The portion of the trail which remains next to the creek is a beautiful place for small children.

After the trail leaves the creek, it climbs steadily upwards via three sets of switchbacks. Just when you think the trees are going to open up for a view, there's another hill and more switchbacks. However, this tall, Lodgepole Pine forest is very quiet and peaceful, and the forest floor has abundant

Heartleaf Arnica greeting the passerby with their cheery faces. The first drainage with reliable water after leaving Summerville Creek is at 10,200'. There are some camping spots in the trees at the right, but there is no view. I recommend continuing to the next drainage which does have a view and some great places to camp. Here at 10,800', you are rewarded with a gorgeous view of parts of Henry Mountain and other unnamed peaks to the north which rise above treeline. The obvious camping area right by the trail is somewhat less than a wilderness camp. I would suggest hiking a short distance downstream into the meadow or following the trail a short distance further and then hiking up the drainage where there are alternative places to camp, as well as two high lakes. It's but a short climb up to the ridge and the peaks above this drainage. From the ridge, it is possible both to look down into the South Lottis Creek drainage, and to see more of the beautiful Fossil Ridge Wilderness.

When Anne Ash and I were returning down the switchbacks on the Summerville Trail, we saw below us, and right next to the trail, a young couple amorously enjoying the solitude. Luckily, I was able to give a loud whistle to warn them that we were coming down the trail.

Heartleaf Arnica

211

SUMMERVILLE TRAIL

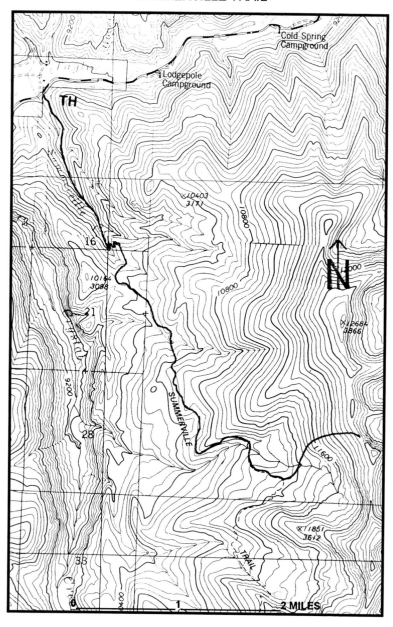

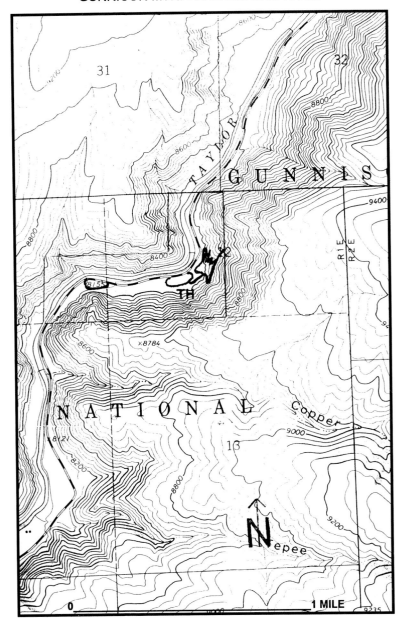

GUNNISON MTN. PARK NATURE TRAIL

USGS Almont
TH Gunnison Mountain Park, Taylor Canyon Road
SE 8200'
TVG 60'
RT .5 miles
EASY

The Nature Trail at Gunnison Mountain Park was created in 1973 by Eagle Scout, Gary Dolezal of BSA Troop #478. He was killed 5 years later in an auto accident when he was 20 years old. Another Eagle Scout, Kevin Doerty, replaced Gary's interpretive booklets with a permanent set of interpretive signs. These signs, which explain both the geology and the plant life of the area, are placed throughout the trail. Gary was assisted by Dr. Thomas Prather and Dr. Sidney Hyde, WSC professors, and Bob Haugen of the National Park Service. On July 30, 1978, the trail was named the *Gary Dolezal Memorial Trail* and dedicated by the City of Gunnison.

Gary Dolezal working on the original trail --Photo courtesy of Ruth Dolezal

TAYLOR CANYON

This short trail is wonderful for children and can be combined with a picnic at Gunnison Mountain Park. The land for the park was deeded to the City of Gunnison from the General Land Office of the United States. The deed, dated May 21, 1927, was signed by President Calvin Coolidge, and it specifies that the land must be used for public park purposes.

Gunnison Mountain Park has two different sections with separate parking areas. The two parking areas are about a quarter mile from each other. When driving from Almont, the trailhead for the Gary Dolezal Memorial Trail is located at the second section of the park. The first section has recently been made to include tent camping, while the second continues to be for day use only.

Wildflowers

Alpine Avens *Geum rossii*
Alpine Clover *Trifolium dasyphyllum*
Alpine Forget-Me-Not *Eritrichium aretioides*
Alpine Spring Beauty *Claytonia megarhiza*
Ballhead Waterleaf *Hydrophyllum capitatum*
Bluebells *Martensia ciliata*
Colorado Columbine *Aquilegia coerulea*
Cow Parsnips *Heracleum lanatum*
Explorer's Gentian *Gentiana calycosa*
Fairy Primrose *Primula angustifolia*
Glacier Lily *Erythronium grandiflorum*
Heartleaf Arnica *Arnica cordifolia*
Indian Paintbrush *Castilleja miniata and chromosa*
Jacob's Ladder *Polemonium pulcherrimum*
Kinnikinnik *Arctostaphylos uva-ursi*
Larkspur *Delphinium occidentale*
Lupine *Lupinus argenteus depressus*
Many-flowered Stickseed *Hackelia floribunda*
Marsh Marigold *Caltha leptosepala*
Monument Plant *Frasera speciosa*
Moss Campion *Silene acaulis*
Moss Gentian *Gentiana prostrata*
Northern Gentian *Gentianella amarella*
Old Man of the Mountains Sunflower *Hymenoxys grandiflora*
Parry's Gentian *Gentiana parryi*
Parry's Primrose *Primula parryi*
Pasqueflower *Anemone patens*
Plumed Avens *Geum triflorum*
Purple Fringe *Phacelia sericea*
Purple Leaf Groundsel *Senecio soldanella*
Pygmy Bitterroot *Lewisia pygmaea*
Red Columbine *Aquilegia formosa*
Rosy Paintbrush *Castilleja rhexifolia*
Scarlet Gilia *Gilia aggregata*
Shrubby Cinquefoil *Potentilla fruticosa*
Siberian Smelowskia *Smelowskia calycina*
Sky Pilot *Polemonium viscosum*
Snow Buttercup *Ranunculus adoneus*

Spotted Saxifrage *Saxifraga bronchialis*
Stonecrop *Amerosedum lanceolatum*
Twinberry *Lonicera involucrata*
Western Spring Beauty *Claytonia lanceolata*
Western Yellow Violet *Viola Nuttallii*
Wild Rose *Rosa woodsii*

TREES

Blue Spruce *Picea pungens*
Bristlecone Pine *Pinus Aristata*
Douglas Fir *Pseudotsuga mensiesii*
Engelmann Spruce *Picea engelmannii*
Gambel Oak *Quercus gambelii*
Lodgepole Pine *Pinus contorta*
Ponderosa Pine *Pinus ponderosa*
Quaking Aspen *Populus tremuloides*
Rocky Mountain Juniper *Juniperus scopulorum*

HIKE RATINGS

The ratings for the hikes were computed on the following formula:

$$VG/M + TM/D + TVG + SE = TOTAL$$

where

VG/M is the vertical gain over the uphill miles divided by 100.

TM/D is the total miles per day.

TVG is the total vertical gain divided by 100

SE is the starting elevation divided by 1000

TOTAL is the sum

HIKE	VG/M	TM/D	TVG	SE	TOTAL
EASY					
Neversink Trail	0	1.5	0	7.6	9.1
Gunn Mtn Park Nature Tr	2.4	0.5	0.6	8.2	11.7
Ohio Pass RR Grade	1	2	1	9.5	13.5
Judd Falls	1	2	1	9.8	13.8
Alpine Tunnel (W Portal)	6	.5	1.5	11.4	14
EASY TO MODERATE					
Ohio Pass Falls	2	2	2	10	16
Beaver Ponds	4	1	2	9.3	16.3
Mill Creek Trail	2.4	2.5	3	9	16.9
Pine Creek Trail	4	2	4	7.2	17.2
Dillon Pinnacles	2.3	4	4.5	7.4	18.2
Beckwith Pass	1.2	5	3	9.6	18.8
Crystal Creek Trail	1.6	5	4	8.5	19.1
Lost/Dollar Lakes	3.2	2.5	4	9.6	19.3
Yule Pass	2	2	4.4	11.3	19.7
MODERATE					
Williams Pass	3.2	2.5	4	11.3	21
Napoleon Mountain	4.2	2.6	5.5	12	24.3
Curecanti Creek Trail	4.4	4	8.8	7.2	24.4
Cinnamon Mountain	5	2	10	11.3	28.3
Powderhorn Lakes	2.2	8	8.6	11	29.8
Coal Mesa Trail	6.1	4	12.2	7.7	30
Mount Poor	5.5	4	11	11.3	31.8
Mineral Creek Trail	2.4	10	12	9.2	33.6
Rough Creek Trail	4	7	14	9.2	34.2
Altman Pass (E Portal)	9.2	2.5	11.5	11.4	34.6
Fairview Peak (Cumberland)	4.1	6	12.2	12	34.3
Rustler's Gulch Trail	3.4	8	13.6	9.7	34.7
Alpine Tunnel Circle	2.9	8.5	12.5	11.3	35.2
Mill Lake	5.8	5	14.5	10	35.3
South Baldy Mountain	4.7	6	14	10.9	35.6
Swampy Pass	3.3	9.5	14.2	8.9	35.9
Cataract Gulch Waterfall	7.1	4.4	15.7	9.6	36.8
Copper Lake	3.8	8.	15.2	9.8	36.8
Cañon Diablo	2.8	10	14	10.3	37.1
Independence Gulch	7.6	4.5	17	8.5	37.6

Lamphier Lake	5.7	6	16.7	10	38.4
Sylvanite Mine	4.2	8	16.5	9.8	38.5
Sloan Lake	7	4.5	15.8	11.3	38.6
Hermit's Rest	6	6	18	8.9	38.9

MODERATE TO STRENUOUS

Purple Mountain	5.6	6	16.8	11.3	39.7
Augusta Mine	4.5	8	18	9.2	39.7
Powderhorn Park	3.5	10	17.6	9	40.1
Summerville Trail	4.4	9	20	8.8	42.2
Matterhorn Creek	6.7	6	20	10.4	43.1
Tumble Creek Trail	3.8	10	19	10.3	43.1
East Maroon Pass	4.6	9.5	19.6	9.8	43.5
Frigid Air Pass	5	8	20	10.4	43.4
Blue Lake	3.6	11	20	9	43.6
Baldy Chato	9.5	4	19	11.5	44
Gunsight Pass	5.4	8	21.4	10	44.8
Mount Baldy	8.4	5	21	10.7	45.1
Cooper Lake	6.1	7.2	22	10.6	45.9
Treasury Mountain	6.3	7	22	11.3	46.6
Ohio Peak	9.1	5	22.7	10	46.8
West Maroon Pass	5.8	8	23	10.4	47.2
Daisy Pass	8	6	24	9.2	47.2
Cataract Lake	6.8	7.2	24.5	9.6	48.1
Fitzpatrick Peak (gentle)	7.6	6.4	24	10.7	48.7
Middle Baldies	4.6	10	23.2	10.9	48.7

STRENUOUS

Mt. Axtell	6.3	8	25.3	9.5	49.1
Carbon Peak	6.4	8	25.6	9.5	49.5
Baldy Cinco	6.7	7.5	25	10.9	50.1
Fitzpatrick Peak (steep)	11	4.4	24	10.7	50.1
Devil's Lake (Deer Lk)	4.2	12	25	10.4	51.6
Angel Pass	6.1	9	27.6	9.2	51.9
Henry Lake	4	13	26	9.1	52.
Continental Divide (Cataract)	6.8	8.2	27.2	9.6	52.3
Crested Butte Peak	7	8	28	9.4	52.4
Marble Quarries	3.4	14	24	11.3	52.7
Alpine Gulch Trail	5.1	11	28	9	53.1
Oh-Be-Joyful Pass (Oh-Be)	4.2	13	27	9	53. 2
Mount Kreutzer	15.8	3	23.8	10.7	53.3
Copper Pass	4.6	12	31	9.8	53.4
Broncho Mountain	5.6	10	28	10	53.6
Avery Peak	9.5	6	28.5	9.8	53.8
Stewart/Cochetopa Loop	4.3	12.5	27	10.4	54.2
Crystal Lake	7.5	8	30	8.8	54.3
North Baldy Mountain	4.8	12	26.9	10.9	54.6
Mt. Bellview	16.7	3	25	10	54.7
Williams Creek Ridge	6.7	9	30	9.2	54.9
Gothic Peak	8.6	7	30.3	9.6	55.5
Stewart Peak	7.5	8	30	11	56.5

Whetstone Mountain	5	12	30	9.5	56.5
Triangle Pass	5.2	12	31	9.8	58
Matterhorn Peak	8	8	31.9	10.4	58.3
Mt. Kreutzer/Emma Burr	10.5	6	31.5	10.7	58.7
Fairview Peak (Gold Cr.)	5.8	11	32	10	58.8
Unnamed Peak (easy)	8.7	7.6	33	9.7	59
Devil's Lake (Powderhrn Lk)	5.1	12	31	11	59.1
Unnamed Peak (steep)	11.4	5.6	33	9.7	59.7

VERY STRENUOUS

Baldy Alto	6.7	10	33	10.4	60.1
Augusta and Mineral Point	6.6	10.5	34.4	9.2	60.7
Grassy Mountain Saddle	4.4	15	33	9.2	61.6
Henry Mountain (Circle)	7	10.2	35	10	62.2
Organ Mountain	5.8	12	35	10.3	63.1
Oh-Be-Joyful Pass (Daisy)	7.7	10	38.4	9.2	65.3
Red Mountain	5.8	13	38	9	65.8
Grassy Mountain	5.8	13	38	9	65.8
3 Pass Circle	5.3	14	36.8	9.8	65.9
Crystal Peak	8.2	10	41	8.8	68
Conundrum HS	6.4	15	48	9.8	79.2

BACKPACK TRIPS					
Storm Pass/West Elk Peak					
Day 1	4.3	6.5	28	9	47.8
Day 2	4.1	6	12.3	11.8	34.2
Day 3	0	6.5	0	11.8	18.3
East Mineral/Skyline					
Day 1	2	6	12	9.2	29.2
Day 2	6	7	21	10.4	44.4
Day 3	0	6	0	10.4	16.4
Tumble/Rough Creeks					
Day 1	3.8	6	19	10.3	39.1
Day 2	0	5	0	11.7	16.7
Day 3	3.3	6	10	10.3	29.6
Mineral/Rough Creeks					
Day 1	2.4	5	12	9.2	28.6
Day 2	5.2	5	13	10.4	33.6
Day 3	0	4.5	0	10.3	14.8
Big Blue/Fall Creeks					
Day 1	2	8.5	17	9.7	37.2
Day 2	6.8	7.3	13.6	11.4	39.1
Day 3	3	7.7	3	11.1	24.8
Tour of the Bells					
Day 1	5.7	6.5	23	10.4	45.6
Day 2	9.2	7	23	10	49.2
Day 3	6.7	6	20	10.9	43.6
Day 4	7	6	14	11	38
3 Pass Circle					
Day 2	8.6	5	21.5	11.3	46.4

Bibliography

Brockman, C. Frank. *Trees of North America*. New York: Golden Press,1986.

Class of 1916. *Historical Sketches of Early Gunnison*. Gunnison, Colorado: The Colorado State Normal School, 1916. (Reprint by Loline Sammons, 1989)

Crofutt, George. *Crofutt's Grip-Sack Guide of Colorado*. Vol. II. Omaha: The Overland Publishing Co., 1885.

Duft, Joseph F. and Moseley, Robert K. *Alpine Wildflowers of the Rocky Mountains*. Missoula: Mountain Press Publishing Company, 1989.

Fandrich, J. W. *The Slumgullion Earthflow*. Lake City Colorado, 1968.

Helmers, Dow. *Historic Alpine Tunnel.* Denver: Sage Books, 1963.

Perry, Eleanor. *I Remember Tin Cup*. Littleton, Colorado, 1986.

Petit, Jan. *Utes The Mountain People*. Boulder: Johnson Books, 1990.

Prather, Thomas. *Geology of the Gunnison Country*. Gunnison, Colorado: Western State College Foundation, 1982.

Spellenberg, Richard. *The Audobon Society Guide to North American Wildflowers*. New York: Alfred a. Knopf, 1988.

Strickler, Dr. Dee. *Alpine Wildflowers*. Columbia Falls, Montana: The Flower Press, 1990.

Taylor, Ronald J. and Spring, Bob and Ira. *Rocky Mountain Wildflowers*. Seattle: The Mountaineers, 1986

Vandenbushe, Duane and Meyers, Rex. *Marble Colorado, City of Stone*. Denver: Golden Bell Press, 1970.

Vandenbushe, Duane. *The Gunnison Country*. Gunnison Colorado: B&B Printers, 1980.

Wolle, Muriel S. *Stampede To Timberline*. Boulder, Colorado: The University of Colorado, 1949.

Wolle, Muriel S. *Timberline Tailings*. Chicago: Sage Books, 1977.

INDEX

INDEX

INDEX

INDEX

INDEX

226

INDEX

I raise my eyes toward the mountains,
From where will my help come?
My help comes from the Lord,
the maker of heaven and earth.
God will not allow your foot to slip;
your guardian does not sleep,
Truly, the guardian of Israel
never slumbers nor sleeps.
The Lord is your guardian;
the Lord is your shade
at your right hand.
By day the sun cannot harm you,
nor the moon by night.
The Lord will guard you from all evil,
will always guard your life.
The Lord will guard your coming and going
both now and forever.
--Psalms 121

Stay Safe